Irish Executive Pres  **W9-BNL-939**

Best Practices in Successful Business:
a collection of tutorials

The Irish Executive Press Authors Group
www.irishexecutives.com

Edited by
Susan Harwood
Doctor in Human Development specializing in the Moral
Psychology of Leadership and Organizational Systems

Published by
Walker Publications
2910 S. Greenfield Rd
Suite 3077
Gilbert, AZ USA

www.walkerpublications.com
ISBN 978-0-9882508-0-2

Contents

List of Contributors   *vi*
List of Figures   *viii*
List of Tables   *ix*
Acknowledgements   *x*
Preface   *xi*

Part One: Best Practices in Launching & Sustaining Your Business

1. **Show Me the Money, Part One: Funding Sources for New Business**
   Gert O'Rourke   *2*

2. Show Me the Money, Part Two: Specific Sources **of Finance for New Business in Ireland**
   Gert O'Rourke   *13*

3. **Tendering: Capturing the Opportunity**
   Adrian Rush   *23*

4. **Build A Startup Team for Execution Intelligence**
   Richard Lawler   *33*

5. **Starting a Business in Ireland**
   John Muldoon   *40*

6. **Starting a Business in Ireland: Market Research and Protecting Your Idea**
   Mary Conneely   *49*

7. **Starting a Small Business**
   Blaise Brosnan   *59*

8. **Creating a Winning Customer Value Proposition**
   Dr. John Fahy   *64*

9. **The Indirect Sales Channel**
Sharmila Wijeyakuma   *73*

10. **How to Make Social Media Work for Your Business**
Zara Sheerin   *82*

11. **Your Marketing and Sales Strategy**
Blaise Brosnan   *93*

Part Two: Best Practices to Achieve Competitive Advantage

12. **Pipelines of Creativity: The Foundation of Continuous Innovation**
Richard Lawler   *102*

13. **GLIDE: Innovation is a Choice**
Dr. Susan Harwood   *106*

14. **Lean: What Executives Should Know**
Dr. Eric Maass   *117*

15. **Design For Six Sigma: What Executives Should Know**
Dr. Eric Maass   *125*

16. **Implementing Cloud Computing Platforms: Running your business on the cloud-is it possible?**
Tony O'Dowd   *133*

17. **Communication: Say it like you mean it…**
Adrian Rush   *140*

Part Three: Best Practices in the Talent Assets of Your Business

18. Talent Development: An Unexploited Dividend
Nial O'Reilly   **147**

19. Glimmer: The Competitive Advantage of Learning
Dr. Susan Harwood   *162*

20. Leveraging Cultural Diversity
Patricia Ryall   *176*

21. Closing the Gaps in Employee Engagement
Imelda McGrattan   *188*

22. Executive Job Hunting
Ken McIntyre-Barn   *195*

23. Time Management: The blueprint to a successful life
Severine Parker   *206*

References   *219*

List of Contributors

Blaise Brosnan
Email: Blaise@mriwex.ie

Mary Conneely
Email: maryconneely@hotmail.com

John Fahy
Email: john@johnfahy.net

Richard Lawler
Email: richard@startinnovating.ie

Susan Harwood
Email: susanlharwood@msn.com

Eric Maass
Email: emaass@gmail.com

Imelda McGrattan
Email: img4sales@gmail.com

Ken McIntyre-Barn
Email: ken.mcintyre-barn@hickskimbermears.com

John P. Muldoon
Email: johnmuldoon@yahoo.com

Tony O'Dowd
Email: tonyatdcu@gmail.com

Nial O'Reilly
Email: nial@ignitecoach.com

Gert O'Rourke
Email: gert@ennisinnovate.ie

Severine Parker
Email: severine.parker@gmail.com

Adrian Rush
Email: amrush@eircom.net

Patricia Ryall
Email: info@duchascoaching.com

Zara Sheerin
Email: zara@mintdigital.ie

Sharmila Wijeyakumar
Email: samw@entando.com

List of Figures

Figure 1.1: Summary Sources of Finance   **7**

Figure 8.1: Customer Value Quadrant   **66**

Figure 10.1 Comparative advertising spend in Ireland   **83**
Figure 10.2 Don't forget about traditional mediums   **85**
Figure 10.3 The Changing Customer   **87**
Figure 10.4 Mint's approach to client campaigns   **89**

Figure 13.1 Glide-ing Continuum   **109**
Figure 13.2 Glide: Balancing Question)   **113**

Figure 15.1 Cellular Phone System   **127**
Figure 15.2 DFSS Flow for Electronic System   **128**
Figure 15.3 DFSS Flow for Software Development Project   **129**
Figure 15.4 Alignment of FADIOU with the DFSS Flow   **130**

Figure 18.1 The Spectrum of Talent Development   **149**
Figure 18.2 Effects of Increased Factor Inputs on Outputs   **151**

Figure 19.1 Glimmer: Organizations as Systems   **166**
Figure 19.2 Glimmer: Foundation Cycle of Change   **169**
Figure 19.3 Glimmer: Learning Organization System Components   **172**
Figure 19.4 Glimmer: Learning Elements of Career Development   **173**

Figure 20.1 Hofstede's Onion Diagram   **180**

Figure 21.1 SWOT Analysis Worksheet   **191**

List of Tables

Table 14.a: Seven Types of Waste   **119**

Table 15.a: Key DRSS Tools and Methods   **131**

Table 20.a: Hofstede's 5 dimensions   **181**

Acknowledgements

In the architecting and editing of the insightful tutorials found within this publication, my respect for each contributor and excitement for the project grew as all the pieces were coming together. The final product is a tangible series of "Business Best Practices" covering a wide spectrum of topics essential for growing enterprises in today's global enterprise.

I realize that often the role of the editor and project manager on a project such as this is to ensure consistency of voice. Instead, I choose consistency of format and retained the unique voice of each writer. Each contributor wrote of personal insights for you from their years of successful professional experiences in their own style.

My thanks to Craig Meek and Simon O'Sullivan of the Irish Executive TV network (a brand offered through POWOW). Their work helped create visual context of the authors and the chapters through the Irish Executive Author Video series on YouTube.

To the founder and President of Irish Executives, John Keogh, my special thanks for his vision. He saw the potential and value of this project for us to undertake as a Social Network Community.

To my colleagues who wrote openly with feeling, insight, enthusiasm, knowledge, and focus, my sincerest thank you. I look forward to working with you on future projects.

Susan Harwood
Editor/Program Manager

Preface

"Every human being has inside them something more important than him or herself – his or her Gift" Paulo Coelho

The Irish Executives Network was founded in June 2008, a time when Ireland and the rest of the world were confronted with grave economic and financial realities. The margin between success and failure narrowed greatly - increasing the need for guidance that businesses could trust and then apply easily to improve business performance and financial outcomes.

The Irish Executives leadership team decided to take action with a unique initiative to share knowledge, wisdom and ideas. We announced the creation of Irish Executives Press at our inaugural summit in Galway, Ireland in 2011. Our goal was to use our social media network to crowdsource aspirational writers and produce a series of books and best practices.

This completed work is proof of what can be achieved through online collaboration and the power of social media networking. It took 6 months of planning, preparation and execution by network volunteers under the inspiring project leadership of Susan Harwood and using Irish Executives TV as a collaboration platform.

This essential handbook provides practical and trusted guidance for companies of all sizes. Compiled from 17 experienced practitioners, subject matters experts and academics, it is divided into 3 core themes covering 23 best practices:

1) Best Practices in Launching and Sustaining your business
2) Best Practices to achieve Competitive Advantage
3) Best Practices in the Talent Assets of your business

The best practices cover critical aspects of business, such as: leadership, talent development, sales and marketing, customer service and product, service and process innovation.

The end result of this exciting journey is a uniquely broad array of insights, based on many backgrounds and even more years of combined experience. We are very excited to present this book and we are convinced that it will appeal to a broad audience, in all stages of business management.

John Keogh
Founder and President of the Irish Executive Network

Part One:
Launching & Sustaining Your Business

1. Show Me the Money, Part One: Funding Sources for New Business by *Gert O'Rourk*

EXECUTIVE SUMMARY

This article aims to describe the various sources of finance that are available to new businesses in Ireland. It reviews the three primary funding sources; government supports, debt finance and equity finance with specific reference to supports at various stages of development. It examines the importance of finance for every new business in the context of the current funding climate in Ireland and considerations for specific funding types. It also discusses the importance and availability of funding for SMEs and the continuous demand for external resources to capitalize on emerging opportunities and support existing business activities. Furthermore the value of using an established business network to seek advice and support and establish the most appropriate source of finance for new business in Ireland will be highlighted.

INTRODUCTION

Congratulations, you have recently set up a new business. You've got a great idea; you've prepared a comprehensive business plan. Now all you need is money. Finance is the life blood of any business. Funding is required from the formation of a business concept, to setting up a business and right through to the growth and expansion stages. Typically in the early stage of new business development funding is sought from personal funds, family, friends, angel investors and debt finance. This paper will provide an overview of the funding supports available to new business which can be categorised into three basic areas; government financial supports, debt financing and equity finance. Finance can be sourced from a number of avenues depending on the size, age and sector of the business and different sources of finance attach different terms and conditions.

Recent research shows that 54% of SMEs are less than a decade old, this is 34% of total SME employment[1]. The importance of supporting young innovative SMEs therefore cannot be understated. As can be seen from the Business in Ireland report 2009, published by the CSO, almost all enterprises are SMEs with only about 500 who are not. Finance is one of the most crucial aspects for these small businesses. They continuously require external support to fund critical business activities and exploit emerging opportunities. The primary options for businesses pursuing external sources of finance are (1) Funding Supports offered by various business support organizations, (2) Debt Financing or (3) Equity Finance. Ireland has a continuously supportive business environment and provides many funding opportunities to those seeking funding for their business. Let's take a closer look at some funding sources available in each category.

As mentioned earlier family and friends are frequently a first port of call for early stage finance. When a young company has more optimism than income, friends and family are often the first to open their check books and provide much needed financial support. They know you and believe in you and your product or service offering. Michael Copeland (2006) warns however of the dangers of taking personal connections for granted. He advises treating friends and family like **business** partners from the outset. For instance, decide up front whether their money will be a loan payable by a certain date with interest or an equity stake, meaning they'll own a percentage shareholding in your new company. Set expectations accordingly, draft legal agreements and make sure it includes provisions such as liquidity preferences i.e. how much an angel is paid before other shareholders if the company is sold and other standard terms like a guaranteed option to invest in future rounds.

Friends and family will also feel less vulnerable if you invest your own savings. At a recent launch of the GMIT New Frontier Program, a support program for startup businesses, the Director and CEO of Irish TV Mairead Ni Mhaoilchiarain commented on her reliance on her own personal funds in the early stages of investment - even the child benefit was invested in starting up her business venture!

Support Funding

Indigenous businesses can raise finance through competing for funding supports from various agencies. Many of these supports are offered by means of a grant whereby successful applicants receive financial assistance in achieving a particular goal or objective. This is perhaps the most beneficial means of raising finance for a new business. Financial supports are available for almost all business initiatives including marketing, research and development, recruitment, expansion, international trade and many more which are outlined in Appendix 1. The most difficult aspect in relation to these support funds is to successfully secure the support most suitable for your business needs. It is often advisable to seek the support of a business advisor who can direct you to the most relevant support for your organization and concentrate on applying for a tailored package of funding supports of specific benefit to your business.

There are various institutions within Ireland that are dedicated to supporting and promoting indigenous business development. These institutions offer a range of business supports in the form of funding, consultation and incubation. Examples include the County and City Enterprise Boards, Enterprise Ireland, Údarás na Gaeltachta and InterTradeIreland. Each of these bodies operate through a number of regional offices throughout the country and business promoters seeking to avail of any of the below supports should contact their nearest regional office.

Debt Financing

In the early years, enterprises often rely heavily on owner's resources and finance from friends and family. As the business matures, profits ensure the sustainability of the firm's cash flow. Given the difficult trading environment of recent years, many businesses have however depleted their cash reserves. Funding the business through debt is an option that involves borrowing money from financial institutions to fund business activities. The acquired finance must be repaid within a set time period and with a specific interest rate. The implications to be considered in relation to debt finance are the effects that repayments may have on the liquidity and working capital of the business. Often an early source of debt finance for a new business is a credit card which could provide enough money to buy furniture, invest in equipment or a marketing campaign. Pay close attention to the interest rate when using credit cards, and pay off as much as you can, or you may thwart your ability to expand. You might be less able to qualify for loans because you have already burdened your credit rating with high-interest-rate credit cards.

A bank is a place where they lend you an umbrella in fair weather and ask for it back when it begins to rain. Robert Frost (1874-1963)

Bank loans can provide a good source of finance for a new business. No matter how good your idea is however you must have a good credit history and well prepared business plan, little debt, solid business experience and usually some collateral to get a bank loan. New business find it more difficult than established ones to source finance and so it is important to have a good relationship with your local bank. Small local banks are usually more likely to support local start-ups and frequently have a dedicated advisor for start-up or expanding businesses. They are more likely to lend you an umbrella in fair weather and let you use it when it's raining. Credit Unions also provide a good source of debt finance. Advice, guidance and assistance on a range of business issues are available through their business support services.

The government is consistently promoting business activity within the country and for this reason many financial institutions now offer favorable terms and conditions to businesses seeking debt finance. There are various forms of debt financing including business loans, overdrafts and asset finance. There are also a number of financial institutions within Ireland offering comprehensive business support packages. One of the key sources of funding for enterprise, the banking system is currently undergoing comprehensive change in terms of recapitalization, deleveraging and restructuring. In March

2011, Bank of Ireland and Allied Irish Bank accounted for 63 per cent of outstanding SME lending in Ireland[2]

Even before the current financial crisis occurred a number of structural issues were evident in the banking sector in Ireland. Innovative exporting Small and Medium Enterprises (SMEs), whose technology and business models are not understood by many financial institutions and lack a track record and collateral against which to raise finance, traditionally experience difficulty in accessing external finance. There are extensive funding tools available from banks ranging from overdraft facilities to innovative debt funding initiatives. According to the Central Bank, given the current economic climate, credit advanced to core SMEs declined by 6.4 per cent in the year ending December 2011. Credit advanced to Irish private-sector enterprises excluding financial intermediation and property related sectors in the year to December 2011 declined by 7.2 per cent compared to a decline of 5 per cent in the year to December 2010 and a decline of 2 per cent in the year to December 2009[3]

But for what purpose do new businesses borrow finance? The Mazars SME Lending Demand Study, November 2011 reflecting the six months to October 2011 showed the most common reasons for requesting new credit were for working capital and cash flow purposes[4] This study shows that trading conditions continue to be difficult, in particular for micro and small businesses. Mazars highlights that trading activity and in particular, profitability has a strong impact on bank loan application decline rates with higher rates of decline associated with poorer profitability levels. The government has attempted to counter the problem of accessing bank finance through initiatives such as the new credit guarantee scheme aimed at assisting businesses access the finance they need and the Microfinance fund aimed at start-up, new or growing enterprises across all sectors, with no more than 10 employees.

Loans of up to €25k are available for commercially viable proposals that do not meet the conventional risk criteria applied by commercial banks.

Equity

Raising capital through equity involves selling off part of the company to third parties and using this finance to fund business activities.

Although this capital does not warrant immediate repayment, there are other implications to be considered such as dilution of control as more shareholders enter the business and dividend payment obligations. Equity financing is becoming increasingly popular throughout the Republic of Ireland as the country moves towards the knowledge economy. Many new businesses are becoming knowledge and technology based and therefore do not have sufficient tangible assets to offer as collateral to financial institutions. Equity finance is therefore a more viable option in such circumstances. Equity investors also bring experience and expertise the management team and research indicates that enterprises availing of equity financing tend to grow faster and turn more profits when compared to competitors.

Equity finance comprises business angels and private investors, venture capital, private equity and government equity. Both CSO and Central Bank data show an increasing percentage of enterprises seeking equity investment and an increased reliance on equity investment. However, there are concerns that potential investors are also facing capital constraints (e.g. venture capital investors) as a result of the economic crises. Figure 1.1 overleaf summarizes the supports available to new business in Ireland.

Figure 1.1: Summary Sources of Finance

Business Concept/Start Up	County Enterprise Board (Priming Grant/Feasibility/Innovation Grant, Mentoring) Enterprise Ireland (New Frontiers Programs CORD Funding/Start Up Funding, Innovation Vouchers/Partnership, Mentoring) Banks (Loan and Start-Up Package, Overdraft, Term Loan, Credit Cards)

	LEADER (Construction & fit-out costs, machinery & equipment, marketing/promotion, certain publications, training, mentoring) First Step (loans up to €25k) Credit Union (Small Business Loan Scheme)
Early Stage Development SME	Banks (Small Business Loan, European Investment Bank loan, Credit Guarantee Scheme) CEB (Business Expansion Grant, Mentoring) Intertrade Ireland (Acumen Program, Microtrade, Fusion, Seedcorn, Business Acceleration Program, Strategic consultancy Grant) Venture Capital (4th VC, ACT, Dublin BIC, Enterprise Equity, Enterprise Ireland, Kernel Capital) Business Angel Investment (Halo Business Angel Partnership) Enterprise Ireland (Feasibility grant, mentoring, internet growth acceleration program, BES) LEADER (Analysis & Development, Construction & Fit out, machinery & Equipment, marketing/promotion, training, mentoring) First Step (loans up to € 25k) Skillnets (Training grant) Job Bridge (Supports a work placement for a period up to 9 months) FAS (Apprenticeship allowance, training, Job Assist, Job Incentive) EU Funding (Eurostars, COST, Competitiveness & Innovation Program)
Developing SME	Enterprise Ireland (Going global grant, International Selling Programme, New Market Research, BES) LEADER (Analysis & Development, Construction & Fit out, machinery & Equipment, marketing/promotion, training, mentoring) Banks (Developing Business Loan, Practice Development loan, Asset Finance) Intertrade Ireland (Acumen Program, Microtrade,

	Fusion, Seedcorn, Business Acceleration Program, Strategic consultancy Grant) Skillnets (Training grant) EU Funding (Seventh framework program FP7) Sustainable Energy Ireland (Accelerated Capital Allowance)

CONCLUSION

There is an array of business funding supports available to new business in Ireland. Whatever financing route you choose, in the long run it must be one that works for you. Starting a business is a very emotional and rewarding move. You are putting yourself, and quite possibly your livelihood, on the line. Pitfalls abound, so make sure you weigh all the options carefully. Your final choice should be the one that gives you the greatest odds of success and suits your personal circumstances at the present stage of development.

There is an abundance of advice and support available through the grant agencies and business development advisors such as the Business Innovation Centers[5] all of whom provide business planning assistance and funding advice. There are many business support programs[6] in Ireland who can support your new business and advice on relevant sources of finance and who in many instances can provide personal introductions to banks, venture capital funds and business angels. In the words of my namesake Gertrude Stein *"Money is always there but the pockets change."* Use your business network to seek advice and source the most relevant source of finance for your new business.

End Notes:
[1] Business in Ireland 2009, CSO
[2] The Financial Measures Programme Report for March 2011 shows Allied Irish Bank and Bank of Ireland accounting for €36.5 billion of SME exposure. Central Bank Business Credit statistics estimate total SME lending at €58.2 billion.
[3] Central Bank (2012) Trends in Business Credit and Deposits: Q4 2011

[4] Mazars (2011) SME Lending Demand Study, November 2011

[5] Gertude Stein was an imaginative, influential writer in the twentieth century and a major patron of the arts.

[6] Business Innovation Centres in Ireland include WESTBIC, Dublin BIC, Cork BIC, Limerick BIC, SEBIC and Noribic.

[7] Examples of Business Support Programmes include Enterprise Ireland New Frontier Programmes (www. enterprise-ireland.com/en/Start-a-Business-in-Ireland/Supports-for-High-Potential-Start-Ups/New-Frontiers-Entrepreneur-Development-Programme.htm) and Ennis Innovate (www.ennisinnovate.ie).

REFERENCES

Agndal H, and Nilsson U. (2009), *Interorganisational cost management in the exchange process*, Management Accounting Research 20: 85-101

Central Statistics Office (2012) *Business in Ireland 2009*

Copeland, Michael V (2006), *How to Find your Angel*, Business 2.0; Mar2006, Vol. 7 Issue 2, p47-49, 3p,

WEB BIBLIOGRAPHY
http://www.forfas.ie/media/260412 The Irish Enterprise Funding Environment-publication.pdf (accessed July 19th 2012)

http://www.djei.ie/enterprise/smes/publications.htm   (accessed July 30th 2012)

http://www.djei.ie/enterprise/smes/RIA_Credit_Guarantee_Scheme.pdf (accessed July 30th 2012)

http://www.enterpriseboards.ie (accessed July 30th 2012)

http://www.enterprise-ireland.com (accessed July 30th 2012)

http://www.first-step.ie (accessed July 30th 2012)

http://www.hban.org (accessed July 30th 2012)

http://www.idaireland.com (accessed July 30th 2012)

http://www.intertradeireland.com (accessed July 30th 2012)

http://www.irishleadernetwork.org (accessed July 30th 2012)

http://www.revenue.ie (accessed July 30th 2012)

http://www.aibseedcapitalfund.ie (accessed July 30th 2012)

http://businessbanking.bankofireland.com/loans/seed-and-early-stage-fund (accessed July 30th 2012)

http://www.ivca.ie (accessed July 30th 2012)

http://www.enterprise.gov.ie/Publications/Financial-Support-for-Irish-Business.pdf (accessed July 30th 2012)

http://www.revenue.ie/en/tax/it/leaflets/it15.html) (accessed July 30th 2012) (Accessed July 30th 2012)

www.revenue.ie/en/tax/it/leaflets/new-it55-e11.pdf (accessed July 30th 2012)

http://www.revenue.ie/en/tax/ct/research-development.html (accessed July 30th 2012)

https://innovationvouchers.ie (accessed July 30th 2012)

http://www.seai.ie/Your_Business/Accelerated_Capital_Allowance (accessed July 30th 2012)

http://www.revenue.ie/en/tax/it/leaflets/it59.html (accessed July 30th 2012)

http://www.welfare.ie/en/schemes/jobseekersupports/backtowork/employerjobprsiincentivescheme/Pages/Emp_PRSI.aspx (accessed July 30th 2012)

http://www.jobbridge.ie (accessed July 30th 2012)

http://www.connectireland.com (accessed July 30th 2012)

http://www.djei.ie/press/2011/20110510d.htm (accessed July 30th 2012)

http://www.djei.ie/press/2012/20120411.htm (accessed July 30th 2012)

http://www.creditreview.ie (accessed July 30th 2012)

http://www.skillnets.ie (accessed July 30th 2012)

http://failteireland.ie (accessed July 30th 2012)

About the Author: *Gert O'Rourke, Training and Development was formed to provide practical business assistance to entrepreneurs, enterprises, support organizations, and community groups. This organization provides tailored support to innovative enterprises and projects from initial concept right through to commercialization and post-launch stages.*

Her development services include feasibility study assistance, market research and marketing planning, business planning, business development advice, strategic development, training and sourcing of entrepreneurial finance/sponsorship.

The 2009 winner of the Marketing Institute of Ireland, West Region Award for Start Up Business; Outstanding achievement award winner for networks and groups, IITD, 2012 & 2010;

Outstanding achievement winner, SCCUL Entrepreneur of the Year Awards 2010 highlights the achievements of Gert's firm creating a path to success for her clients.

Gert holds an MBS in Financial Services from Michael Smurfit Graduate School of Business and a Bachelor's in Commerce from the National University of Ireland.

2. Show Me the Money, Part Two: Specific Sources of finance for new business in Ireland by *Gert O'Rourke*

EXECUTIVE SUMMARY

This article provides an overview and links to sources of **finance** accessible to small and medium size enterprises (**SMEs**). **SMEs** form an important part of private sector in Ireland but often encounter difficulties accessing external finance, hindering their development plans. Specific financing tools available to SMEs are mentioned here and can be useful in facilitating growth. As mentioned in an earlier article, *Show me the Money - funding sources for new business*, finance for companies can be categorized into three basic areas; government financial supports, debt financing and equity finance. The following is a sample list of sources of business funding and business support services in Ireland. This is a summary list which is not comprehensive and funding sources should be reviewed directly with the relevant authority to ensure up to date information is available.

Accelerated Capital Allowance
(www.seai.ie/Your_Business/Accelerated_Capital_Allowance)
The Accelerated Capital Allowance (ACA) allows companies to write off 100% of the purchase value of qualifying energy efficient equipment against their profit in the year of purchase.

Back to work enterprise Allowance
(www.welfare.ie/en/schemes/jobseekersupports/backtowork/enterpri seallowance/Pages/ea.aspx)
If you have been signing on for over 12 months and you would like to become self-employed, the Back to Work Enterprise Allowance (BTWEA) allows you to keep your social welfare payment for 2 years (Year 1: 100%, Year 2: 75%). To qualify, you must be setting up a business that a Local Integrated Development Company or a Facilitator has approved in writing in advance.

A short-term Enterprise Allowance can be claimed by anyone who has lost their job and who is eligible for Jobseekers' benefit. It runs until your Benefit payment would have expired.

County Enterprise Boards
(www.enterpriseboards.ie)
There are 35 CEBs established in Ireland in 1993 to provide support for small businesses ('micro-enterprises') with 10 employees or less, at local level. CEBs provide direct grant-support to new and existing enterprises and promote entrepreneurship, capacity building and women-in-business at local level, to micro enterprises in the commercial sphere. The CEBs support both new and established businesses with a suite of supports including business advice, mentoring, grant aid and supports for training and growth

Credit Guarantee Scheme
(www.djei.ie/press/2012/20120411.htm)
The Credit Guarantee Scheme facilitates €450m of additional bank lending over 3 years to viable micro, small and medium enterprises to help them obtain the working capital and investment that they need. The Government provides the lender with a 75% guarantee for which the borrower pays a 2% premium. Target companies are those lacking adequate security for a normal commercial loan, or where bank understanding of the specialized aspects of the business environment in which they operate is limited.

Credit Review Office
(www.creditreview.ie)
If you're a small business, sole trader or farm owner who has had difficulty getting credit or loan facilities of up to the new €500,000 limit or you have had an unfavorable change to your existing credit terms, get in touch with the Credit Review Office for an independent review. The banks are required to comply with the recommendation or to give their reasons for not doing so to the Credit Review Office. The Office has overturned the Banks' decision in 35% of cases to date

Employer Job PRSI Incentive Scheme
(www.welfare.ie/en/schemes/jobseekersupports/backtowork/employ erjobprsiincentivescheme/Pages/Emp_PRSI.aspx)

The Employer Job (PRSI) Incentive Scheme is open to employers who create new and additional jobs.

Under this scheme, employers do not have to pay the employers' portion of the PRSI contribution for 18 months subject to certain criteria.

Employment and Investment Incentive Scheme
(www.revenue.ie/en/tax/it/leaflets/new-it55-e11.pdf)

The Employment Investment Incentive (EII) has replaced the Business Expansion Scheme and provides tax relief for investment in certain corporate trades. The maximum investment by all investors in any one company or group of companies is €10m subject to a maximum of €2.5m in any one 12 month period. It allows individual investors to obtain income tax relief on investments up to a maximum of €150,000 per annum in each tax year up to 2013. Subject to certain restrictions for high income earners, relief is initially available to an individual at 30%. A further 11% tax relief will be available where it has been proven that employment levels have increased at the company at the end of the holding period (3 years) or where evidence is provided that the company used the capital raised for expenditure on research and development.

Enterprise Ireland
(www.enterprise-ireland.com)

Enterprise Ireland is the state agency responsible for supporting the development of manufacturing and internationally traded services companies. It provides funding and supports for companies - from entrepreneurs with plans for a high potential start-up through to large companies expanding their activities, improving efficiency and growing export sales. Funding and supports for college based researchers to assist in the development; protection and transfer of technologies into industry via licensing or spin-out companies are also available.

Fáilte Ireland
(www.failteireland.ie)

Fáilte Ireland is the National Tourism Development Authority. It's role is to support the tourism industry and work to sustain Ireland as a high-quality and competitive tourism destination.

It provides a range of practical business supports to help tourism businesses better manage and market their products and services. It also works with other state agencies and representative bodies, at local and national levels, to implement and champion positive and practical strategies that will benefit Irish tourism and the Irish economy.

First-Step Micro Finance
(www.first-step.ie)
First Step provides loans of up to €25,000 to people who want to create their own enterprise and who cannot access funding, or sufficient funding, from other sources. First-Step's core goal is to help finance start up and expanding Small and Medium Enterprises (SME's) to provide job opportunities. First-Step has an application and screening process which evaluates the applications received and stress tests them for likely success based on information received. First-Step is a private not-for-profit company. It receives funding from Enterprise Ireland through the EU Seed and Venture Capital Fund and the Social Finance Foundation. First-Step is the beneficiary of an SME Guarantee Facility created within the framework of the Competitiveness and Innovation Framework Program (CIP) of the European Community.

Halo Business Angel Partnership
(www.hban.org)
Halo Business Angel Network (HBAN) is an all-island umbrella group for business angel investing in Ireland. It is focused on creating Angel Investor syndicates across Ireland. The network aims to link individual angel investors or investment syndicates with companies seeking funding of up to €250,000+ per investment. Investors have extensive business acumen and industry experience which can help accelerate the growth of the business. Investment criteria include;
- A product that is ready for commercialization.
- Pre-revenue is considered however some early market traction via revenues preferred.
- A management team with relevant experience.
- An identifiable market opportunity.
- An internationally scalable business model.

IDA Ireland
(www.idaireland.com)
IDA Ireland (Industrial Development Authority) is responsible for the attraction and development of foreign investment in Ireland. It is focused on securing investment from new and existing clients in the areas of High End Manufacturing, Global Services, Research, Development and Innovation.

Innovation Vouchers (www.innovationvouchers.ie)
If you own or manage a small limited company and you have a business opportunity or problem that you want to explore, you can apply for an Innovation Voucher worth €5,000. The objective is to build links between Ireland's public knowledge providers and small businesses to create a cultural shift in the small business community's approach to innovation.

Intertrade Ireland
(www.intertradeireland.com)
InterTradeIreland is an organization which supports SMEs across the island to develop North/South trade and business development opportunities for the mutual benefit of both economies. It encourages better use of our collective resources to accelerate trade and business growth across the island and create an environment where it is easier to do business. Inter-trade Ireland can assist through a range of business support program and through a co-operative business policy and research program, partnerships and networks.

Irish Venture Capital Association (IVCA)
www.ivca.ie
IVCA is the representative organization for venture capital firms in Ireland. IVCA contributes to many expert groups, advisory committees and other consultative bodies, which are involved in advising Government Departments, the European Commission and others about the venture capitalist views on many issues. IVCA represents its members at international level through its national membership of the European Venture Capital Association (EVCA)and works closely with all other European national bodies. Members of IVCA include ACT Venture Capital

www.actventure.com, ETV Capital www.etvcapital.com, Novus Modus www.novusmodus.com, NCB Ventures Ltd www.ncb-ventures.com , Delta Partners Ltd www.delta.ie , Fountain Healthcare Partners www.fh-partners.com, Growcorp Group Ltd www.growcorp.net, Kernal Capital www.kernalcapital.ie, AIB Seed Capital www.aibseedcapitalfund.ie Dublin Business Innovation Centre www.dbic.ie , Seroba Kernal Life Sciences www.seroba-kernal.com 4th Level Venture University Seed Fund Ltd www.4thLevelVentures.ie, Western Investment Fund www.wdc.ie

Leader Group See www.cldc.ie as an example of a Leader group
The Irish Leader Network is a network of 36 Local Action Groups dedicated to the promotion of sustainable rural communities and the preservation of rural fabric, providing the highest quality of services to rural people. Its primary aim is to act in union with member groups and with other relevant interests to promote innovative models for local integrated rural development and to shape new policies at Irish and European level to underpin these models. The following categories can benefit from Leader Funding:
- Rural Businesses wishing to expand or diversify, or a newly established business
- Farm Families wishing to diversify into non-agricultural activities
- Community Groups promoting community enterprise, local amenity projects or community services
- Voluntary Organizations or special interest groups promoting social, cultural and environmental projects
- Partnerships promoting projects in collaboration with other organizations

Micro Finance Fund
(www.djei.ie/press/2011/20110510d.htm)
The Government has developed a Microfinance fund aimed at start-up, new or growing enterprises across all sectors, with no more than 10 employees. Loans of up to €25k are available for commercially viable proposals that do not meet the conventional risk criteria applied by commercial banks.

Applicants will have to demonstrate that they have been refused credit by a commercial lending institution before their application is considered. The new fund will generate €90m in new lending to 5,500 micro enterprises which will support 7,700 new jobs. Borrowers will pay a commercial interest rate.

Revenue Commissioners
(www.revenue.ie)
The Revenue Commissioners provide tax relief and tax refunds for new and existing businesses who meet established criteria. The Seed Capital Scheme (SCS) for example in conjunction with its associated scheme, the Business Expansion Scheme (BES) are tax relief incentive schemes. The BES provides tax relief for investment in certain corporate trades, while the SCS provides for a refund of tax already paid by an individual, when that individual sets up, and takes employment in, a new qualifying business (as defined). Both schemes have broadly taken the same format over a number of years and, because they are a form of State-aid (at the level of the enterprise), any changes to the scheme require the approval of the European Commission, to ensure that it remains compatible with EU law.

Revenue Job Assist
(www.revenue.ie/en/tax/it/leaflets/it59.html)
Revenue Job Assist offers both employers and workers an incentive where people who have been 12 months or more on the live register (or disability allowance) are recruited. The employer gets double write-off of the wages plus employers' PRSI for 3 years – even at the minimum wage, it is worth €2,500 per year to a company and up to €8,000 per year to a sole trader. The worker gets an extra tax allowance of €3,810 plus €1,270 for each child in year 1 and two thirds of these allowances in year 2, one-third in year 3. For a worker on the 20% rate it is worth at least €762 in the first year, or €1,524 over the three years.

R&D Tax Credit
(http://www.revenue.ie/en/tax/ct/research-development.html)
The R&D Tax Credit is a valuable tax-based incentive designed to encourage investment in R&D by companies in Ireland.

A 25% tax credit for qualifying R&D expenditure exists for companies engaged in qualifying R&D. This credit may be set against a company's Corporation Tax liability. The first €100,000 of all qualifying R&D expenditure will benefit from the full 25% R&D tax credit from 2012. It is particularly of benefit to SMEs. For larger R&D expenditure, the tax credit will continue to apply only to the amount by which expenditure in 2012 exceeds that incurred in the base year 2003. The total tax benefit of qualifying R&D expenditure is 37.5% when in addition to the tax credit you take into account the normal 12.5% corporation tax deduction for the expenditure.

Seed Capital scheme
(http://www,revenue.ie/en/tax/it/leaflets/it15.html) If you start up and work full-time in your own company, you can claim back the income tax you paid in the previous 6 years to invest equity into a company (subscribed as shares) engaged in a qualifying trade. The amount of relief is restricted to the amount of the investment. Since November 2011, the scheme is open to a much wider range of sectors. The ceiling on recoverable tax can now be up to €100,000 in each of the 6 look back years.

Three Year Corporate Tax Exemption
This scheme provides relief from corporation tax on the trading income and certain gains of new start-up companies in the first 3 years of trading. There will be full relief on income and gains relating to the trade where total corporation tax liability in any of the first 3 accounting periods does not exceed €40,000. There will be marginal relief where the tax liability falls between €40,000 and €60,000. You can earn €120,000 tax free per year for the first 3 years

Job Bridge
(www.jobbridge.ie)
Job Bridge offers an internship of 6-9 months to a person who has been signing on as available for work and getting a payment or credits for at least three months. Time completed on program in FÁS training, back to education or on a community scheme will count towards eligibility. Participants receive €50 per week on top of their welfare payment.

Skillnets

(www.skillnets.ie)

Skillnets is a state funded, enterprise-led support body dedicated to the promotion and facilitation of training and up-skilling as key elements in sustaining Ireland's national competitiveness. It supports and funds networks of enterprises to engage in training under the Training Networks Program (TNP). These networks, now referred to as 'Skillnets', are led and managed by the enterprises themselves to design, manage and deliver specific training programs across a broad range of industry and service sectors nationwide. Businesses can avail of subsidies for up-skilling employees. Training is also provided for job-seekers, who are training with those in employment.

Succeed in Ireland

(www.connectireland.com)

Succeed in Ireland rewards people who introduce potential foreign investors to Ireland. Through an online referral network, introductions can be made that will lead to new jobs in Ireland. The person that makes the introduction will be financially rewarded after a period of time of the jobs coming to fruition. The reward runs from €1,500 to €3,000 per sustainable job.

About the Author: Gert O'Rourke, Training and Development was formed to provide practical business assistance to entrepreneurs, enterprises, support organizations, and community groups. This organization provides tailored support to innovative enterprises and projects from initial concept right through to commercialization and post-launch stages.

Her development services include feasibility study assistance, market research and marketing planning, business planning, business development advice, strategic development, training and sourcing of entrepreneurial finance/sponsorship.

The 2009 winner of the Marketing Institute of Ireland, West Region Award for Start Up Business; Outstanding achievement award winner for networks and groups, IITD, 2012 & 2010;

Outstanding achievement winner, SCCUL Entrepreneur of the Year Awards 2010 highlights the achievements of Gert's firm creating a path to success for her clients.

Gert holds an MBS in Financial Services from Michael Smurfit Graduate School of Business and a Bachelor's in Commerce from the National University of Ireland.

3. Tendering Best Practice by *Adrian Rush*

EXECUTIVE SUMMARY

This Best Practice for Tendering is to give those not involved and to those involved in tendering some pointers to keep them on track whilst tendering. All the points are based on experience and years of preparing tender responses. It is to show what should be done to achieve the best results and the processes by which to get them. It also outlines some general rules and principals for the presentation of Tender Responses which is aimed at increasing a tenderer's chances of being successful.

INTRODUCTION

This Best Practice for Tendering is going to highlight the major points to consider when looking at Tendering and responding to tenders. Tendering is a specialized form of Technical Writing and as such has its own rules and guidelines. Why should a company of any size consider Tendering? The aim of tendering is to produce a document that the potential client wants to open and read. Tendering has several functions in business – one is a response to a special request by a new or existing client or government agency or department. Secondly it is an unsolicited way of introducing your company to a potential new client. It is essential that your presentation is of the highest quality and I would recommend working to BS 4884 for your template as it will give you a clear and readable response.

THE BUSINESS OF TENDERS

Sources of Tenders
There are several sources of tenders.
- Virtually all countries have a web site that advertises the government tenders and in fact many more companies are starting to use the same site.
- In America there are three types of tender and these are Federal, State and Government.

- In Europe each country has its own system but they are very similar especially for EU Members, some charge to be a member of the site and some do not, either way you can register and either have alerts sent to you weekly or go to the web site and look for yourself.

- Some large organizations such as the World Bank, UN and European Bank for Reconstruction and Development have a tender section on their web site, the EU also has a tendering section on its web site. With all of these you can register and check yourself or have alerts sent to you.

- The EU Journal is another source of tenders and you have to pay to receive it. In the EU there are various threshold limits and these are available on the individual country web sites.

- You can also find tenders in the major papers but this practice seems to be dying out.

- There are some specialist companies that you can register with and if you give them a set of industry/business sectors they will search for you and send you the details; it will cost a significant amount of money for something that a company can quite easily do for itself.

Reading and Understanding the Tender Request
It is essential that before committing pen to paper or typing a single word, you fully and completely understand what the tender is asking. If you have any questions it is very important to ask them of the Tenderer.

When you have read the Tender several times it is always a good idea to highlight (with a yellow highlighter) the important parts of the Tender Request. The more you read it the better you will understand what the potential client is looking for. It is essential to go through the Bid/No Bid Questionnaire.

This will clear up any reservations a company may have about going for the Tender (Proposal).

Note: Should you decide to go for the tender what are the important things to remember

Due Date:

- I always work to at least two or three days and sometimes a week before to allow time for review and changes.
- Order that response has to be supplied in

Success Tip: This may sound very silly but you will lose if you have the costs as section 3 when it should have been section1.

Questions:

- You have not answered all the questions that are asked or completed and signed all the forms correctly.
- Number of copies and soft copy:

Success Tip: More often these days a potential client is asked to submit their response using an electronic post box on the web site that advertised the tender request.

Supplied all information or made a statement concerning the supporting information which you intend to supply should you be selected, giving reasons why it is not in the Tender Response.

Template and Contents
In many cases a potential client will not ask for the response in a particular order. So you can use your own company Template. I recommend that all companies should have a tender response template.
Your template should be flexible and yet unique. How is this achieved well it is actually very simple.

Every Tender Response should have the following pages.
- **Front Cover**
- **Title Page**
- **Contents Page**
- **Executive Summary**
- **Introduction**
- **Methodology**
- **Costs**
- **Project Team**
- **Project Plan**
- **Appendices**

Success Tip: If you are sending your Tender Response by post or courier it is essential to put in the envelope a **Covering Letter**

Having designed your template it is now time to turn to the contents. When responding to a tender request it is most important to be factual and never ever be vague. You may well be answering to a series of questions that do not look like questions – but believe me they are.

Front Cover

Always give you Tender (Proposal) a front cover it makes it look more professional and complete. A front cover should always be used even if you are employing the simplest of binding methods. The front cover should have the exact title of the project from the Tender Request. You can put a photograph of client's offices or something relevant to the project as a background or around the words and if you can I would suggest putting the potential clients logo on as well. This has to be thought about at a very early stage so you can get it finalized and any printing started as quickly as possible.

Title Page

The title page should have the same title as the front cover (maybe slightly smaller text), your company logo and services or address. It should also have the main and an alternative contact for your company.

Contents List

The contents list is a complete list of the contents of your response to the tender request. In a simple one volume tender response do not go further than first level heading and page numbers. This would also apply to more complex tenders but if you are producing a very complex response I would suggest going down to second level headings and unless it is absolutely essential going no lower down. If you have a lot of figures, diagrams, tables and photographs it is very important to list them

Executive Summary

This is not always required and should only be used if asked for. An Executive Summary is there for exactly what it says on the tin – it is for Senior Executives to read so all they want is an overview or outline of the tender response and how it is going to solve the potential client's problem. Never ever put the cost into the Executive Summary.

Introduction

This is a brief outline of your business, your experience and I always put in things like Business Registration Number, VAT (or similar for other countries) Number, here is the best place to highlight any Assumptions you have made and to put any Compliance Statements asked for by the Tender Requestor. Also if you are in a Consortium, Joint Venture, or Group, each member is introduced in the Introduction with a brief outline of each company. Sometimes you can add a page before the contents list (I have done on a couple of occasions), this page is a table showing each Companies Logo; Company Name; Person responsible to contact for this proposal, contact information and finally you can add a column showing which sections of the tender or project each member of the team is responsible for.

Methodology

How your company is going to solve the problem, design, build the building design and implement the new software package or carry out the work asked for in the Tender Request.

This has to be very detailed and at the same time a little vague so as not to give away too much confidential information.

If you include information that is company sensitive – it is essential that you highlight it and also mention this in the covering letter or e-mail. The approach to take essentially depends on the industry and exactly what is being asked for from the potential client. *I will talk briefly about Project Plans in a later paragraph.*

Depending on the industry will determine how you respond to the Tender Request; also watch out in the Tender Request Document for a special order of the response, this does happen and you must without fail follow it. Now work your way through each phase or part of the project and answer it clearly, fully and comprehensively. Responding to each item and making sure you have answered as fully as possible. Do not be afraid to insert diagrams, figures or photographs into your response but make sure you number them properly and you talk about each one immediately after it in the response.

If you are working in a Consortium, Joint Venture or Team give each of them a realistic but as tight as possible writing deadline. Depending on the size and practicalities it might be worth having everyone in one place say at your offices for the duration of the preparation of the response. However you manage it you have to remember you have to work on your colleague's material when you have received it. Drawings, diagrams, photographs or figures have to be commissioned as soon as possible because they take time to produce or source; if any work is required on them when you get them you will need time.

If during your deliberations and design of the solution you come up with alternatives ideas from the outline given in the Tender Request. You can add to the Methodology an alternative solution to the client's request. This will show that you can think outside the box and are a forward thinking company. This would always be the last part of your Methodology.

Cost
This is often the most discussed and changed part of any tender response. Depending on the type of project there are a few ways to cost your response. The simplest method and mostly used for simple projects is a Project Cost. This is made up of:

- A daily rate for staff working on the project.
- An hourly rate for staff working on the project.
- Additional Costs – this can include travel accommodation, attending meetings, stationary and telephone calls.
- Net Cost
- Contingency – It is advisable to put one in so if there are changes during the project you have some cover and if major changes happen you should ask for it to be added as a variation. The amount of contingency really depends on the overall cost of the project.
- Value Added Tax (or any other Government Tax levied on work or services) at the appropriate rate.
- Grand Total

Some projects the client will give you a Pricing Schedule and essentially you fill this in making sure you complete every single part of it. Remember your contingency and tax before you complete the grand total section.

If a project is divided up into phases simply work out the price for each phase and I suggest you include your Additional Costs on a phase by phase basis. Complete the costs for all the phases and then show each phase cost and the put in your Net Price and remember your contingency and tax before you complete the grand total section.

If you are working in a Consortium, Joint Venture or Team show each companies cost separately under the appropriate sections and have each of their Additional Costs shown then the total net price followed by the contingency and tax and then the complete grand total for the project.

Project Team
This section is for you to show who you plan to use on the project. Make sure you give the client Curriculum Vitae (Career Summaries). In a lot of tender responses these days you will be asked for a Brief

Summary for each person. If you are asked for full versions make sure they all look the same (same format). There is nothing worse than submitting a response with many different styles of Career Summary it is horrible. It is a good idea to include a passport size photograph of you prospective people as well, many people react to a picture better than words.

If you are working in a Consortium, Joint Venture or Team the first thing to decide is who is going to act as Lead Company and then how the rest link into that. An Organizational Chart will have to be drawn up to show who is responsible for what section of the project. The client should designate a project manager but if they do not I would suggest at the very top of the Organizational Chart putting one to show the line of responsibility.

Project Plans
These are not very often asked for unless the project is a long duration project. The best way to draw one up is using specialist software. If one is asked for on a short duration project I would suggest using something like Excel and just putting in the key dates.

Appendices
In here you put all the additional information you are asked to supply such as Accounts or Account Summaries, References, Quality Assurance Certification, Health and Safety Statement, Quality Assurance Statement, List of Client for similar work, Letter from Bank (only if asked for), if you have them you can include one page samples for similar projects, you can also include one page samples for different projects to show your companies diversity.

Covering Letter
If you are sending you response by post or courier you will need to write a Covering letter. Address it to the person who you have to send it to and give it the same title as the response. The body of the letter should say what you are sending in and if you have made any assumptions mention them in the letter again. Do not be smooth or effusive in the letter it will put the potential client off.

One of the last things connected to the preparation is the tab dividers between the sections. Be unique yes fine but do not go over the top.

If you have to sub divide in a section use colored paper and type the title of the sub section on to it and make sure you instruct the printer correctly.

Managing Tender Response

Managing a Tender Response is not difficult but I would also add it is not easy either. The difficulty will depend on the complexity and size of the response. A simple response can easily be managed using tables in MS Word. Complex ones can be managed using MS Excel. There is no real need to use expensive project management software for a tender response. Whatever you use you must make sure you have each section listed, the name of the person responsible and when it is due to reach you as the Proposal Manager.

I have found it is best to put in the due dates for the individual sections and the date you actually received the section. Do not forget to put in a section for the Front Covers, Folders, Dividers and the date you have asked for them and keep pressure on your printer/supplier because they like the rest of the response have to be checked and reviewed.

CONCLUSION

In conclusion Tendering is hard work and stressful. I would recommend all companies look at it as a way to get new clients. If you have never attempted a tender before look for a company that specializes in that type of work and let them guide you through the process. There are also courses available on tender preparation so it would also be worth considering attending one of them and some colleges in Ireland have evening classes for the subject.

Above all I would say tendering is worth the effort, hard work stress and late nights because you never know you might win the contract. This is true for your Micro Business up to your multi - national conglomerate every company has to tender for something at some point. Tendering is definitely worth it because as I say to people I meet who tell me they are reluctant to tender "if you are not in you will not win". Have a go surprise yourself and win!

About the Author: *Adrian Rush is a respected seasoned professional the Documentation/Publications Industry. As a qualified Project Manager, Technical Writer, and Editor, his company, AMR Enterprise serves divers multi-national companies in the area of Documentation Consultancy. His clients include British Aerospace, Gilligan Black Recruitment, UTS Parking and Transportation, Hewlett Packard, Pfizer European Financial Shared Services, and Meteor Mobile Communications.*

Most recently, Adrian's focus has been in successful Tender Response and writing a series of Handbooks for running successful businesses. As the Proposal Manager for a LinkedIn Group, his Tender Response Template was the basis for pursing a major project in Shannon.

Adrian attended Wycliffe College Stonehouse Glos England
www.amrenterprises.net

4. Build A Startup Team for Execution Intelligence by *Richard Lawler*

EXECUTIVE SUMMARY

This article offers a sneak preview of a new publication due out in November 2012 on building your entrepreneurial startup team. The article encourages entrepreneurs to focus on their team when starting a business and the requirements needed to give the best chance of success.

The best practices included are **the need for execution intelligence, understanding the number of co-founders needed** and the **choosing of mentors.**

* A single arrow is easily broken, but not ten in a bundle.
- Japanese proverb

* None of us is as smart as all of us.
- Ken Blanchard

INTRODUCTION

We as a society are moving beyond the one person startup and are now well into the team of a minimum two or three people within the founding team. You don't have a choice but to build a team, get over it. Building your team, the right team is a difficult task perhaps more difficult then you first expected.

You want to build a team that has the best chance of survival and a team that investors might want to invest in, regardless of where the money to startup is coming from you or an external source.

"When investors evaluate a start-up company, they report about 25% of the final decision is based on the team" which is another reason to bear in mind who is on your startup team even before you consider looking for investment.

Criteria used by VCs to determine if a startup is fundable have been employed in this paper. It could be asked do VCs know what makes a fundable team in reality; however the assumption here is that they have some idea based on successes to date. It may be the case that you are an outlier and your college roommate is the perfect choice and that none of this applies to you - the best of luck with that.

A well rounded team with execution intelligence
Execution Intelligence (ExI) is what makes one team fundable and another not, is what marks one team for success and the other for failure. ExI looks at your team and asks what is their knowledge of the space, how is the teams chemistry, what is their experience and the team's ability to work well together. A combination of these factors helped teams survive in hard times.

In essence it is a well-rounded team that can cope with the twists and turns of a pressure cooking rapidly accelerating roller coaster knife fight with scars of past battles.

The following are the criteria to look for: **Domain Knowledge, Fast growth scar tissue, Experience in hyper competitive markets, Risk management skills, the experience profile of the entire team** and **leadership know how** when building a team for ExI.

- **Domain Knowledge**, how well does the team know the area into which they plan to enter?
- **Fast growth scar tissue**, You must have someone on board who has in the past lead a fast growth startup
- **Experience in hyper competitive markets,** have you been up against companies who wanted to kill you? Find someone who has driven a team in this situation.
- **Risk management skills**, keep probing customer pain and be alert to changes that that might shift the market against you.
- **The experience profile of the entire team,** marketing know-how, product development, sales leadership all of these will be required.

- **Leadership know how,** have you built strong teams in the past and been able to hold them together through hard times.

The above should give your insight into what it takes to build execution intelligence and a well-rounded team. Other factors to consider around team characteristics are: **industry experience, leadership experience, managerial skills,** and **engineering/technological**.

Professor Nikolaus Franke identifies four additional team characteristics – **level of education, type of job experience** (start-up vs. large firm), **age,** and **mutual acquaintance within the team** – as important to get funding and therefore important to success of the entrepreneurial startup.

Action point! Take the above points and map out on a white board what you have and what you are missing. Even if you think your team is complete already you may well find that you have gaps, which will need to be addressed. Looking at the missing areas and create a number of action points to resolve this gap.

How many founders does a startup need?
As was touched on already if you want to grow and build a world class company you will be starting off with a small team. In a recent interview with startup expert Dan Feeney we discussed this issue:

> *"Startup teams should have the right mix of business and technology if the company is an internet platform. About 60% business and 40% tech/programming seems about right. A blend of youthful idealism and aged wisdom is also important. The founder/idea person should have stamina, perseverance and the capacity to fail fast and continuously iterate the platform."* Dan Feeney, Startup Business Expert

Professor Nikolaus Franke in his research talks about when they reviewed business plans four was about the size of the core startup teams. So if you are asking do I need a co-founder for my startup the answer is yes – time to move on and get over it.

Finding a co-founder

When you have figured out which kind of cofounder you need then you need to know how to select the right one. You want to find someone you won't clash with, someone who works as hard as you. You're not looking for an employee this is not a 9- 5 venture. Perhaps you have known them for a while do they answer the phone on the weekends? Or vanish of the face of the earth.

Become Friends First Find out about who they really are. Ask them questions about ethical situations. Find out how they treat people? Remember you want to treat your staff with respect. Under pressure back against the wall how to they treat people?

Test the Relationship

Can you do some kind of work with them initially to see what they are like? A small project perhaps? Could you find someone you worked with before in a past role what might be suitable?

Pick a Good Match

Skill sets should be complementary, not redundant. Team members have to work on their own on different areas of the business. Two sales men might have divergent view where as one sales man and an IT guy might be a better match as they are doing complementary jobs.

Clarify Your Position

Sit down and have a discussion about what is happening in each of your lives. It would be interesting for you each to complete a five-year personal, life and career plan. Then compare it are you both going in the same direction.

No early days NDA's it screams you are stuck or over invested in the product. To quote one VC it says, "I'm clueless". It puts up major red flags and warnings. This indicates you have not thought about the value of the team in its execution and not considered the customer.

Initial Alternatives to Co-founders

In the very early days as you are looking for cofounders you can still move forward. If you are looking for a tech co-founder in 2012 there is a significant demand and so it might take longer than in other years as an example. Alternative include learn to code yourself or hire an external team.

Using external sources to develop a minimal viable product (PMV) could be one way to get money coming into the organization, which might then attract a co-founder on the technology side.

Action Point! Determine which of the co-founders you are and which other founders you need. There are entrepreneur meet up nights held in most towns and often this is a good place to find a co-founder. Don't tell them what you want to build but what you are building it will give you a better chance of getting someone else on board. One such group is Entrepreneurs Anonymous http://johnmuldoon.ie/entanon/

Choosing a Mentor

First time entrepreneurs with gaps in their skill set are best to seek out and get assistance from experienced entrepreneurs either as board members, mentors or investors. They will bring on board the execution intelligence already spoken of. You need to ensure that you are getting what you want out of the deal and are not going into it starry eyed.

Mentors past success: You have seen them speak at conferences and read papers they have written; Ask them to tell you of examples of their success, ask did they really contribute to the success of a previous venture or where they just along for the ride. Don't let their success intimidate you and prevent you from due diligence.

Mentors connections: Find mentors who can open doors for you, people with contacts in the key places you need to get into. Test them and see that they are not just hot air and can actually deliver meetings.

Mentors personality: Can you work with this mentor and can they work with you as part of your team? Speak with people they have worked with in the past as mentors and see if you really can depend of this person to take your call when you need them. Can they offer ideas as well as accepting ideas being rejected from time to time?

Action point! Develop an action checklist for hiring mentors. Don't be intimidated by "fame". Have they taken any mentors training courses to really learn to mentor correctly?

CONCLUSION

Building a startup team is hard work and I have just given you a taste of what you are in for, but if you are going to do it you might as well do it right. This article offers a sneak preview of a new publication due out in November and some action points to get you started with build your team.

I challenge you to sit down and think about execution intelligence and how you are going to get it for you entrepreneurial startup. If you're not interested in getting execution intelligence on your team you're likely not interested in success.

REFERENCES

Nikolaus Franke, Venture Capitalists' Evaluations of Start-Up Teams: Trade-Offs, Knock-Out Criteria, and the Impact of VC Experience.

http://cynthiakocialski.com/blog/2010/09/16/why-few-start-ups-build-the-fundable-dream-team/

About the Author: Richard is a cross-disciplinary change agent focused on intrapreneurship coaching clients in the areas of Innovation, Creativity and New Business Launches. Both inquisitive and open-minded, seeing around the corner and thinking laterally are Richard's value adds. Collaboratively and diplomatically, he designs sustainable Win-Win scenarios. Mentally, he is perceptive, nurturing, and supportive.

*These factors make him suitable for the 21st Century Knowledge Economy as a thought leader.Author of **Innovation Demystified: Tapping into your creative core**.*

Irish Executive Press

Richard holds a Master's Degree in Business/Entrepreneurship and Bachelor's in IT Management from Dundalk Institute of Technology. For a consultation please email - richard@startinnovationg.ie

5. Starting a Business in Ireland by *John Muldoon*

EXECUTIVE SUMMARY

There are a number of ways to start a business in Ireland. This article guides the prospective entrepreneur through each of those and discusses the advantages and disadvantages of each approach. While there are common themes throughout, some approaches will work better in some industry segments than others.

INTRODUCTION

Starting a business requires hard work and homework. You will need to do a lot of research, a lot of networking, and a lot of experimentation. Against all that comes some very sound advice to keep your start-up *lean*. Lean does not just refer to holding on to your precious start-up cash. It also calls for economy of effort as you bring your product or service to market. The key with lean start-ups is to validate your offering with real customers before you sink too much time and money in to developing a product that could go on to fail in the marketplace.

Before the bubble burst, I returned to Ireland from America. I had been working in IT for 10 years at that stage and was eager to set up on my own. With an idea imported from the States that I was sure would work here, I took a FÁS course to introduce myself to the business world.

Boy, was that a mistake. Although the idea required serious capital, I allowed myself to be talked out of it by not one, but two, industry veterans. It would never work here, they assured me. Less than a year later, my idea sprang to life when Dublin saw the launch of two identical offerings. Although different in key respects to my plan, someone else had exploited the same opportunity.

I was vindicated, but still a wage slave. Now, after finishing an MBA, networking studiously in Dublin's start-up circles, and after finding a business partner and a (new) workable business idea,

I can share some of what I have learned and perhaps take a year or so off your entrepreneurial preparations.

Lesson 1 and 2: Your Gut and Your Team

The first lesson is to listen to your instinct. If starting your own business is something you always wanted to do, then figure out how to make that happen. The first two things you will need are an idea and a team. While a lone entrepreneur can take on the world, that person is unlikely to have the mix of skills needed to excel in each key area of the business. And studies show that the failure rate of sole practitioners is alarmingly high compared to two- or three-person teams.

The next thing is your idea. Don't be precious about it. No one is going to "steal" it. In fact, chances are that it has already been dreamed up elsewhere. The sad fact is that ideas are a dime a dozen. The real questions are: How are you going to make your concept compelling? Why would people buy your version over your competitors?

As for a giant multinational stealing your idea, the odds are close to zero that will happen. Their dirty little secret is that they are risk averse. Despite all their talk about innovation, no one will put their career on the line for what could ultimately be a flop. What the company might do, however, is approach you with a purchase price once your start-up proves to be viable.

As for Non-Disclosure Agreements (NDAs), they are viewed with disdain in many quarters. Venture Capitalists (VCs) will run you out the door if you ask them to sign one. Their logic is that they are not going to invest in a secret. You are going to have to talk about your idea to people eventually. They key is to keep working on it to bring it to reality. However, you may develop Intellectual Property (IP) that should be protected. This will be hard to protect if your business is web-based. It is also expensive to file patents, but it may make strategic sense to do so.

Although your business idea and strategy may seem like sublime genius to you, the market may think differently.

So, in addition to all the other variables and uncertainties inherent in starting a business, you will have to factor in changes of direction. These are known as "pivots" in the current jargon and, in fact, start-up guru Eric Ries recommends that new businesses hold pivot meetings every six weeks or so to determine if strategic change is warranted. Failure to do so, he argues, can result in a business blindly following an unworkable idea and burning through irreplaceable start-up cash and time.

This brings us to the key challenge facing potential start-ups. Where does that money come from? There are a number of sources and each has its own advantages and drawbacks. For the moment, however, let's split them in to two groups: Government agencies and everyone else. We'll put government aside for now and look at the other options available.

Bootstrapping

The term "bootstrapping" comes from the notion of pulling yourself up by your bootstraps. You put the money in, then you work without pay, most likely from home. Precious cash is kept by deferring outlays or bartering and generally being creative with what little cash you have. It's tough and it may mean working a second job or living off one income if married. But the upside is that you maintain 100% ownership of your business.

Friends and Family

If you can convince enough of your circle of family and friends of the merit of your idea, they might be willing to invest. The advantage here is that they may be easy to persuade. The downside is that if your business fails, relationships could take a hit and you could find yourself still listening to snide remarks about the €200 Uncle Joe lost on your "pie in the sky scheme." Also, if your circle includes knowledgeable investors, they may demand an equity stake in your business.

Crowdfunding

A relatively new arrival on the scene is the slew of websites such that attempt to match entrepreneurs with potential investors.

Kickstarter.com is probably the best known international example. But in Ireland, we have FundIt.ie and Seedups.com. Some crowdfunding sites target certain industry sectors so look around to see which suits your needs best. It may be tough to raise the necessary cash off these operations, so prepare a Plan B.

Accelerator Programs

If you are looking for more structured funding options, accelerator programs are worth a look. The good news is that Dublin has three of Europe's Top Eight, according to the Kauffman Fellows. That's no mean feat for a small country and is a reflection of the vibrancy of the start-up scene in the country. The accelerator programs run once or twice a year, and hold competitive calls where finalists are invited in to pitch their proposals before a panel.

The schemes run for three months usually, although new arrival Wayra will start a six-month program later this year. They expect entrepreneurs to work full-time on-site on their projects, and will pay the teams some money to help cover expenses. While there, the programs provide mentoring from experienced entrepreneurs and, crucially, invite angel investors and VCs to meet the teams. In return, the programs take an equity stake in the business. The NDRC, for example, takes around 6.5% for providing up to €20,000 over its three-months. Wayra plans to take 10% for the €50,000 it provides over six months.

These programs run at different times of the year so it is worth keeping an eye open to see when they are accepting applications. The primary challenge with these programs is that investment is unlikely to be forthcoming during or immediately after your stay in the incubator. That means looking for other sources of income. It should also be noted that the programs focus on customer validation and market research over product development. So if you have a tech guy on your team, they might find that frustrating.

Angel Investors

Angel investors, or just "angels," are high net-worth individuals who are willing to invest in your start-up in return for an equity stake. Although the concept has matured in America, it is still relatively new in Ireland.

However, the scene is organizing and a number of syndicates have formed. The advantage of a syndicate is that the investors can spread their risk by investing in a number of start-ups. For the entrepreneur, it allows them to tap in to a wider network of contacts and expertise.

The downside, as usual, is that the investors will want equity in your business. It is also worth noting that the investors will look very carefully at the teams before them. They may do some background research, but they will certainly look closely and unemotionally at your team and business model. If anything does not add up, or if they suspect information is being massaged or withheld, they will walk away.

Conversely, the entrepreneur should look closely at what the angel brings to the table. The start-up team should not accept money just because it is offered. They need to be confident the investor can provide domain expertise and industry contacts.

The best way to meet angels is through networking. However, a successful spell in an accelerator program that has led to the acquisition of your first customers will certainly help your prospects with potential investors.

Venture Capital
Unlike angels that invest their own cash, VCs are companies that manage investment funds on behalf of large clients like pension funds. They typically invest larger amounts after the seed funding rounds have taken place. There are almost two dozen venture firms in Ireland that specialize in industry sectors like healthcare, IT or green tech. Their approach is more organized and structured than the one taken by angels.

For example, once a potential opportunity has been identified, the VC will perform extensive due diligence on the start-up. This could include background checks, IP research, market analysis, competitor analysis and so on. This work could take several months to complete and makes for an anxious wait for the entrepreneurs until the deal is confirmed.

VCs will want an equity stake and will want at least one representative on your board of directors.

Their shares will take preference over everyone else's, and it is at this point that the angel investors will be bought out or see their equity stakes diluted.

Both VCs and angels will be looking for a substantial return on their investment through an "exit" event like an IPO or sale of the company. They are not interested in funding "lifestyle businesses" where the owner makes a modest living just because he wants to be self-employed.

Banks
Although typically viewed as a source of cash, banks in Ireland are experiencing both liquidity and solvency problems at the moment. Their risk tolerance is likely to be extremely low. Needless to say, starting a new business is inherently risky. The banks, however, do manage cash through their own venture operations. Examples include AIB's Kernel Capital.

Government
Government, by its nature, is bureaucratic and process driven. And by process, I mean their process and not anything likely to be found in the market place. In contrast to the lean and "fail fast" approaches taken by the accelerators, government agencies are likely to ask for a lot of form filling. One of the key differences between the two approaches is in business planning. Start-up accelerators will use something like the *Business Model Canvass*, a one-page planning document. This is in recognition of the fact that very early stage companies can only guess at what their revenues are likely to be in a year's time. Government agencies, however, take a more traditional approach and ask for business plans that project out income and expenses up to three years.

However, the different agencies are worth talking to. The City and County Enterprise Boards are a good first stop. In addition to funding opportunities, they run many training and networking events for small businesses. These may be of more worth outside Dublin where there is not the critical mass available to support different meet ups.

Enterprise Ireland (EI) concentrates on larger firms. Although EI will invest in conjunction with VCs, its success metrics are based on jobs and export potential. It is typically reluctant to take the lead in investing and instead leaves the job of valuation up to the VCs. EI will then add additional funding and will also take an equity stake.

Keep It Lean
Lean is the new buzzword in start-up circles. In industry it is associated with efficiency and process improvement. Kaizen, developed in manufacturing environments in Japan, focuses on the "7 wastes." This is an effort to reduce things like time, materials or defects in the production of goods. At first, it may seem like an unlikely concept to apply to start-ups. After all, they are lean and resource poor by definition. But fledgling firms often waste time and effort developing products, services or websites that fail to find a market.

The lean concept, as applied to start-ups, calls for them to test their products frequently and honestly in front of potential customers. If it is determined that the offering has no future, then the company should drop that product, revisit its strategy and "pivot" to another potential offering. The goal is to find something the market will embrace before the start-up runs out of "runway" — the cash reserves that pay the bills until customers start buying your product.

Know Thyself
Entrepreneurship is a compulsion, maybe even a mental illness. Entrepreneurs want to do it, even if they don't quite know what "it" is. But starting your own business is hard and statistically likely to fail. Entrepreneurs know that, mitigate the risks and plough ahead. If they fail, they try again. If the idea is bad, a good entrepreneur will modify or ditch it. If the execution was bad, a good entrepreneur will learn from his or her mistakes.
These behaviors require a certain personality — someone who is comfortable assessing risk and comfortable with ambiguous and fluid situations. According to the Ernst & Young study, *The Personality Characteristics of Ireland's Most Successful Entrepreneurs*, those starting a business have:
- A proactive, take-charge style

- Self-motivation
- A competitive edge to get things done
- A positive response to pressure and challenge
- An ambition for achievement and
- An impatience and dissatisfaction with routine.

Interestingly, the study found entrepreneurs are not necessarily outgoing but adopt that behavior because they feel it is necessary. The bottom line is "know thyself." If you would rather take a pay hit than work for a boss, then entrepreneurship is for you.

CONCLUSION

There are a few ways to approach starting a business. However, all have a few things in common: Build a strong team, be ready to adapt and conserve resources. Meanwhile, those resources can come from a number of sources. You can fund the business yourself. If more cash is required, you can reach out and ask family and friends to invest. If, for whatever reason, that does not work, you can follow more formal routes of resourcing. These include Accelerator Programs and work on up through Angel investors, Venture Capitalists or government agencies. Each has its own advantages and disadvantages. The entrepreneur should evaluate each option carefully before committing.

REFERENCES

Fund & Follow Creativity [Online] (2012) Available: http://www.kickstarter.com/ (last accessed Aug. 28, 2012).

Gruber, F. (2011) *Top 8 European Startup Accelerators And Incubators Ranked: Seedcamp And Startup Bootcamp Top The Rankings* [Online] Available: http://tech.co/top-8-european-startup-accelerators-and-incubators-ranked-seedcamp-and-startup-bootcamp-top-the-rankings-2011-06 (last accessed Aug. 28, 2012).

O'Leary, P (2009) 'The Personality Characteristics of Ireland's Most Successful Entrepreneurs', unpublished, Trinity College Dublin.

Ries, E. (2011) *The Lean Startup: How Today's Entrepreneurs Use Continuous Innovation to Create Radically Successful Businesses*, New York: Random House.

About the Author: *John Muldoon is an IT professional with a strong interest in innovation, management, and technology, especially web development. He is a board member of Raidió na Life, an Irish-language radio station in Dublin, is adjunct lecturer at the NCI, and organizes a monthly entrepreneur meet-up ("Last Tuesday") in Dublin.*

John achieved an MBA at the Dublin Institute of Technology (DIT) where his dissertation was on Venture Capital in Ireland. You can read more of John's writing on entrepreneurship and company funding at his blog at http://www.johnmuldoon.ie. His Twitter handle is @JohnPMuldoon

6. Starting a Business in Ireland: Market Research and Protecting Your Idea by *Mary Conneely*

EXECUTIVE SUMMARY

This article is designed to provide potential entrepreneurs with information on 2 areas which impact on starting a new business in Ireland: (1) How to Get Started with Your New Business and (2) How to Protect Your New Business Idea. There are other significant issues to consider when starting a business in Ireland and I hope to cover these in future articles.

How to get started with your new business looks at the research which should be undertaken by prospective entrepreneurs and the resources available in Ireland for this type of research. This section discusses the importance of knowing the size of your potential market, its location, and your competitors and provides Irish and international sources for this information. Some tips for pricing your product and forecasting sales are also discussed. Finally this section looks at various supports for new businesses in Ireland including mentors and incubation centers. Protecting your new product or idea gives a general overview of intellectual property principles including patents, trademarks, copyright, and design protection.

INTRODUCTION

The downturn in the Irish and world economies has left many people out of work and unable to find jobs in which their skills and experience will be utilized and appreciated. For some people becoming an entrepreneur may be the answer. This article addresses some of the major issues faced by people trying to start their own business in Ireland.

Becoming an entrepreneur usually starts with an idea for a product or service. Once you have your idea, you have to determine if it is economically viable. The big question is – will this new product or service make money?

Luckily Ireland has a lot of information and structures in place to guide you through the process of determining whether or not there is a market for your product or service.

HOW TO GET STARTED WITH YOUR NEW BUSINESS

Market Research – Size and Location

Your first step to determine whether your idea is economically viable is market research. This research is not as complicated as it may sound and a lot of the information you need is either freely available or available at a low cost. Your research should be focused on 4 elements:

- Size and location of your market
- Pricing of your product or service and your profit margin
- Your competition
- Sales forecasts

You must determine who the potential buyers for your product or service are. You need to research how many potential buyers currently exist and also make reasonable predictions on the number of future buyers. For example, if you were designing a new type of child car safety seat, you could reasonable assume that your main customers would be parents of babies and small children. So you would need to find out how many babies/young children are in Ireland already as well as what the population trend is for births in Ireland.

Your first stop for market size in Ireland is the website of the Central Statistics Office (CSO) at www.cso.ie. The CSO compiles statistics on the Irish population, various industries, employment, salaries etc. The CSO website has information on the 2011 census already broken down into various tables and reports and if a particular demographic isn't already included in a CSO report, you can use the CSO's databases to calculate it. Additional statistical information for Ireland is available from the Economic and Social Research Institute (ESRI) as well as individual government departments.

If you think your product may have export potential – that you will be able to sell it outside of Ireland, you need to look at market statistics for your target export areas. You should explore market statistics for the UK, Europe, America or even Asia. In most other countries or regional areas you will find the agency charged with compiling statistics for that area by doing an internet search. For example in the UK, there is the UK Statistics Authority whose website www.statistics.gov.uk would be a starting point for market research there and in the United States there is the US Census Bureau and its website www.census.gov.

Additional information on market share can be derived from specialty publications and websites such as Kompass (www.kompass.com) and Dun & Bradstreet (www.dnb.co.uk) which include international business information. There are also companies which will do market research on your behalf for a fee. If you need to keep your initial costs down, you should be able to compile relevant statistical information to use for market share assumptions by doing the research yourself.

You have to decide whether to focus on the Irish market or include other markets. Remember that you can always launch your product or service in Ireland and then expand into other markets at a later date. If you are considering marketing your product outside of Ireland, there are additional factors to consider determining your potential profit margin. These factors include:

- Transportation costs
- Distribution costs
- Possible need to open an office or subsidiary in that market
- Costs of complying with laws and regulations in another market
- Taxation issues

Pricing and Profit Margin
What to charge for your product or service is often a difficult question for new entrepreneurs. If you charge too much, customers won't buy your product or pay for your service.

If you charge to little, you may not make enough money to sustain your endeavor. A good way to begin researching your price point is to assess what your competition charges for similar products.

Even if you think your product or service is unique, there are more than likely similar products and services already in the marketplace.

Do some general internet searches and try and find what type of competition exists. You can find detailed information on products on patent databases (www.epo.org, www.uspto.gov, www.patentsoffice.ie). Detailed company, product and market information is also available at varying costs on market research databases such as www.marketresearch.com. (Clients of Enterprise Ireland can access various market research databases at its Information Centers.) Pick out the top 2 or 3 competitors and study their products' features. Look at the prices of your competitors' products and evaluate their products' pros and cons. Also consider the quality of competitors' products (in person if possible) and check if the products were reviewed anywhere such as www.amazon.co.uk, *Which,* or *Consumer Reports.* Compare your product to your competitors – what does your product do that your competitors' products don't or what does your product do better than your competitors.

You also have to decide what the main selling point is for your product and make sure your price reflects this. If you want to pitch your product as the best quality product in a range of products, your price point needs to reflect this quality. If you want your product viewed as the bargain product in the range, your price needs to be lower than your competitors.

You must also calculate the production cost of your product. Your calculation should include all costs associated with the production. At some later point you may be able to reduce your production costs but for now take what it actually costs you at present. The difference between the selling price of your product and the cost it takes you to produce it is your gross profit margin. Your gross profit margin is a significant factor in determining the future profitability of your venture.

There is no magic formula for determining the right price for a product, but by researching the competition, knowing how you want consumers to perceive your product and knowing your production costs you will be able to determine a reasonable price point.

Forecasting your sales

With a new business or product, forecasting your future sales is difficult as you have no direct sales history to go on. You may think I have a great product why do I have to bother with sales forecasting. As a new business, you will probably seek funding from a financial institution or investors. As part of this funding process, you will have to prepare a business plan with key financial information and predictions and you cannot do this without forecasting your sales. Additionally before you invest a lot of your own time, effort and money, you need to know that ultimately you are likely to make a profit.

Forecasting your sales is actually just making an educated guess. You have already looked at your competitors' prices so now you can look at their sales as a starting point to forecasting your own sales. You should also look at consumer buying trends. General information on consumer sentiment is readily available on government websites in Ireland and internationally if you do an internet search. Information on consumer trends enables you to determine if a market is growing and allows to you make assumptions about sales growth which you can include in your sales forecast.

Mentors

A mentor is an invaluable resource for new entrepreneurs. A mentor is an experienced business person who can provide you with guidance, information and advice at any point in your new venture. Enterprise Ireland has a mentoring program which is available at a low cost to high potential start-ups and other small to medium enterprises. (www.enterprise-ireland.com). Most city and county enterprise boards also have panels of mentors available at a low cost to people hoping to start their own businesses There are also private companies which offer mentoring services at varying prices.

All reputable mentors will sign confidentiality agreements so that you can share your business ideas openly with them.

Networking

Many people underestimate the power of networking. When you are starting a new business, networking provides you with:

- Potential customers
- Potential referrals
- Wisdom from other experienced entrepreneurs
- Other professionals to bounce ideas off of and get advice from
- Business Contacts

Although much of the business world is on-line now, there are still plenty of opportunities to do face to face networking. You will find networking groups and events through your local chamber of commerce, the Irish Small and Medium Enterprises Association, industry associations and other regional groups. You should constantly strive to build your network of contacts as you never know when you might need assistance or an introduction from a contact. Make sure you get contact details/business cards from anyone you meet at networking events. Plan to send a note or email a week or so after the networking event to the contacts you met. Your goal is to stay in contact with the people you meet and nurture your relationships.

On-line networking is another useful way of building your network of contacts. Linked In is the most popular site for business networking. Linked In affords you the opportunity to join groups which may be of interest to you and/or your business. Groups range from those set up for alumni of various colleges and universities to those set up for people with a connection to a country such as Irish Executives. Join groups and actively participate in group discussions to expand your network of contacts. There are also groups on Facebook and Google which you can join.

Incubation Centers

Incubation Centers are business centers set up to help people starting a new business. Many new business ventures need somewhere to use as a base in their early stages. Incubation centers offer low cost office space and facilities to entrepreneurs.

By using an incubation center, you can avoid having to pay high overhead costs for office rental or having to sign an extended lease before you get your business off the ground. The facilities on offer vary depending on the incubation center you use but may include desk space, meeting rooms, internet access, reception facilities etc.

Many universities and institutes of technology in Ireland have incubation centers. You need to contact the organization in your area to find out what they offer and what their requirements are. Some City and County Enterprise Boards offer, or are affiliated with, incubation centers which can be used by their clients.

PROTECTING YOUR IDEA

Many people with a new business or product idea are afraid to share their idea in case someone else decides to use it. At the early stages of researching your potential business, this concern can be addressed by simple confidentiality agreements. As you progress with your idea, you will need to consider getting legal protection for it.

What is Intellectual Property?
In simple terms, intellectual property is the legal protection of your idea. Intellectual property law offers legal protection to designs, inventions, logos, brands and artistic work. There are four main elements:
- Patent
- Trademark
- Copyright
- Design Protection

The applicable law depends on the jurisdiction and depending on your product or idea you may need to apply for legal protection in Ireland and/or in other countries or regions.

In Ireland, the Irish Patents Office (www.patentsoffice.ie) is where you apply for a patent, trademark or design registration. You can apply for intellectual property protection individually in other countries, at www.uspto.gov for the United States Patent
and Trademark Office or for regional protection in the European Patent Office at www.epo.org. Applying for intellectual property protection outside of Ireland will be costlier and you may need the assistance of a patent agent or lawyer.

Patent

A patent confers upon its holder, for a limited period, the right to exclude others from exploiting (making, using, selling, importing) the patented invention, except with the consent of the owner of the patent. (www.irishpatents.ie)

A patent gives an inventor legal protection over her invention for a limited time which is usually for 10 or 20 years. This protection keeps others from using your idea. You can only obtain a patent on a new, inventive process or product.

Trademark

A trade mark is the means by which a business identifies its goods or services and distinguishes them from the goods and services supplied by other businesses. (www.irishpatents.ie)

A trademark essentially protects branding. You see trademarks every day, the Coca Cola logo, Mr Tayto and McDonald's golden arches are all examples of trademarks. If you want to create a uniquely identifying logo for your new company, you may want to apply for trademark protection. Trademark protection can last forever.

Copyright

Copyright is the legal term, which describes the rights given to authors/creators of certain categories of work. Copyright protection extends to the following works:
- original literary, dramatic, musical or artistic works,
- sound recordings, films,
- broadcasts, cable programs,
- the typographical arrangement of published editions,
- computer programs,
- original databases. (www.irishpatents.ie)

Copyright protection is automatic and you do not have to apply for it. If you create something that falls into one of the categories above, you are the creator and are protected by copyright law. This © is the symbol you should use on your creations to assert copyright protection. Copyright protection usually lasts for a substantial number of years. In Ireland, copyright protection can last from 50 to 70 years. (www.irishpatents.ie)

Design Protection

"Design" means the appearance of the whole or a part of a product resulting from the features of, in particular, the lines, contours, color, shape, texture or materials of the product itself or its ornamentation. (www.irishpatents.ie)

Design protection acts as legal safeguard over the physical appearance and visual elements of your product. Protection is only given to new designs with "individual character" and the protection applies to designs on paper as well as 3 dimensional products. Design protection is usually given for a limited number of years initially but can be extended upon application. (www.irishpatents.ie)

CONCLUSION

Starting a new business can seem daunting but there are plenty of resources and supports in place to help you determine if your idea can develop into a successful business. One of the most important things you can do is research your market and competitors. This research is critical as it helps you determine at an early stage whether or not you should proceed with your idea or whether you need to refine it before expending more of your resources. Starting your own business is a lot of work but the rewards of being your own boss and watching your business.

REFERENCES

www.irishpatents.ie
www.patentsoffice.ie
www.uspto.gov
www.epo.org
www.enterprise-ireland.com
www.marketresearch.com
www.patentsoffice.ie
www.kompass.com
www.dnb.co.uk
www.statistics.gov.uk
www.census.gov

www.cso.ie

About the Author: Mary Moynihan Conneely holds a Bachelor of Arts Degree in Journalism, Politics and Government as well as a Juris Doctor from Suffolk University Law School in Boston. Prior to relocating to Ireland in 2001, Mary worked as a litigation attorney at a prominent law firm in Boston.

Her first entrepreneurial start-up in Ireland was a successful construction firm. She also served on the board of directors of a credit union, board of management of a primary school and treasurer of a pre-school service
Mary launched Connemara Business Services in 2006 to provide a range of business consulting and accounting services to companies in her area. Utilizing her extensive experience in law, advocacy, negotiation, training, finance and government, her company provides a one stop shop to assist small businesses in financial, legal and technical areas

She does voluntary advocacy work in medical and educational issues affecting disabled people and serves as a parent liaison for the Special Needs Parents Association in Ireland and is active in a local disability group.

7.   Starting a Small Business by *Blaise Brosnan*

EXECUTIVE SUMMARY

The critical messages contained within this Article will facilitate you to get your business beyond this "tipping point" and you should then start to feel the winds more to your back than hitting you on the face.

" There is very little relationship between business success and sweat. You have to work smarter rather than harder"

INTRODUCTION

Starting a new business is a bit like trying to get the fly-wheel of a compacting machine to start turning. Initially it requires a big burst of engine power to get it spinning. From that point forward a lower level of engine power will keep it spinning, as its mass will give it continuing momentum. Your new business will have many head-winds blowing into its face, as you initially travel the steep learning curve of becoming a business person. Provided you have access to the necessary supply of "juice" and are resilient enough to stay at it until your business reaches beyond its "tipping point", then you are likely to build a successful commercial business.

"No man is an island", neither is your business. Business has to initially exist and then succeed within its trading environment. This trading environment tends to go in cycles, with its many peaks and dips. Many businesses are currently going through a dip which appears to be very deep, but this is because of the height that they have fallen from.

The one certainty about cycles is that every peak is followed by a dip and every dip is followed by a peak. It is always difficult to call either the top or the bottom of the market. This is where good judgment calls about future trends come into play. Your effectiveness at making these calls will have a far bigger bearing on your future commercial success than working harder at your current job.

Greed contributed to getting us into this "mess", but we are also depending on greed to get us out of it and onto the next upward cycle. In any market there are the early adaptors, who are eventually followed by the "herd". I believe that these early adaptors are already starting to snap up value out there. Their greed instinct, which is necessary for forward investment and progress, is starting to fuel these initiatives. Eventually the "herd" will start to follow and thus a new "bubble" will be born. The problem is if you are part of the herd, then you cannot go any further than the herd. In markets by the time the herd arrives, it is already too late.

SUCCESS DEFINED

Successful business people are always looking to optimize their Return on their Investment (ROI). They achieve this by building a business model which is reflective of the changing mood of their targeted market. Instead of bitching and moaning about its changing dynamics, they are excited about developing strategies to exploit the emerging opportunities.

Successful business entrepreneurs tend to have the following profile. If you were to score yourself 1 to 10 (with 1 being weak and 10 being very strong) what would your score out of 80 be?

1. Clarity of purpose.
2. Confident.
3. Charismatic.
4. Focused.
5. Energy.
6. Impatient.
7. Assertive.
8. Smart at getting the planned output

What are the messages here for you?
You need a peripheral vision in order to spot new business opportunities. To keep it performing at a high level day to day, you need intense operational focus. When new threats or opportunities emerge on the periphery of their usual business environment, most fail to notice them or misinterpret their importance.

They have a hard time with the weak and ambiguous signals that are often the early warning signs of impending change. Canaries were once regularly used in coal mining as an early warning system of toxic gases. You too need to have your canary equivalents in order to "suss" out the emerging opportunities and threats out there in your targeted market area.

There are many examples of business failures and missed opportunities, where the Business Model wasn't reflective of the emerging market mood. How many second and third generation businesses (other than farming) do you know in your locality? Why so few?

As an operations person, you always face the temptation to focus in on the current fires combusting in your domain. Someone has to do this and giving unwavering attention to operations will often pay off in short-term performance. However by zeroing in on what's in front of you, you naturally lose peripheral vision—and that can threaten your commercial long-term possibilities. Economist describes this as the Opportunity Cost of keeping your head buried in your current job.

A vigilant attitude is the most important trait of business people that are good at anticipating and exploiting change. They search beyond the boundaries of prevailing views.

We all get blinded in our everyday environments. If you want to develop "another business", then you must consciously decide to scan for possible opportunities. You need to look at this as an investment in your future rather than an expense.

- Would you borrow money to go to relevant foreign trade shows in order to spot opportunities?
- Would you invest some of your time resource and scarce money to attend relevant training programs or networking events in order to get a different perspective?

Clarity of purpose is by far the most important ingredient in your future commercial success. It is very difficult to have a sustained burst of energy if you are not sure what you are trying to achieve. Running faster down the wrong road will not get you to your commercial destination. You need to be on the right road.

From your observations and market research you need to clarify:

1. Who is your target market going forward?
2. What relevant need/demand have they that you can more precisely satisfy than your competitor?
   a. Don't fall into the trap of trying to be all things to all people.
   b. Differentiate your "offering" in a meaningful way in order to give your business the edge.
3. Then decide your Action Plan on HOW you will deliver your solution at a price point which will give you your required ROI. The initial steps may be.
   a. Prototype development, protection of intellectual property (IP) and delivery model.

I believe that you as a potential business person must understand that you have to professionally manage your business as per the following two time frames;

1. During the current dip.
2. Post the current dip.

Your style of management, the strategies, and tactics you need to adopt should be different for both phases. You have two choices as follows;

1. Put your head in your hands and use all the negativity out there as an excuse for your poor performance.
2. Start to manage the variables you do have control over and get out there and make it happen.

CONCLUSION

Everything has a price. Are you prepared to pay the price necessary to get your "other business" up and running commercially?

About the Author: During his distinguished tenure as CEO of WFC, Blaise built the business from a humble baseline to become a multi-million business. In 1995, he launched **Management Resource Institute (MRI-**www.mriwex.ie**).** This business specializes in a range of interrelated services including business consulting, management training and commercial mediation services. His practical understanding of the dynamics of management equips him to make **meaningful interventions** for global clients at various stages of the "life-cycles" of their businesses.

In 2008 he launched his first book, **<u>You are the Limiting Factor</u>**, is a management resource book. His second book, **<u>Jack-business lessons from life, life lessons from business</u>** contains "nuggets of wisdom" reflecting our reactions to life issues.

Blaise holds a Bachelor's Degree in Agricultural Economics from UCD and a Masters in Management

8. Creating a Winning Customer Value Proposition by *Dr. John Fahy*

EXECUTIVE SUMMARY

For today's enterprises, building an effective value proposition has never been more important. What research and practice is increasingly showing is that there are just four primary forms of customer value that firms can choose to offer namely, price value, performance value, emotional value and relational value. This article explores the nature of these four types of value in detail and demonstrates that sustained success requires leadership on one of these dimensions. The challenge is not an easy one but the experience of world beating firms from around the globe suggests that it is worth striving for.

INTRODUCTION

Back in 1980 in a small part of the Swiss consumer foods giant Nestle, an innovation project was reaching fruition. Engineers had been trying to develop a machine for brewing fresh gourmet coffee and their efforts would ultimately lead to the multi-billion dollar business that is Nespresso today. But the journey was far from plain sailing. The nascent venture nearly died more than once. The product was originally launched in the restaurant market where it failed to catch on. This was followed by an attempt to penetrate the office market which once again had limited success. These early efforts are far removed from the sophisticated brand that Nespresso is now, embodied by the suave personality of George Clooney and the coffee experience of its department store boutiques. What Nespresso did was to incrementally work out and implement a powerful value proposition that over two decades eventually brought them sales measured in billions, high profits and sustained growth averaging 20 per cent year on year during the recession-hit noughties.

For today's enterprises, building an effective value proposition has never been more important for several reasons. Most global industries are extremely competitive. Innovations are rapidly duplicated and competitors can appear from anywhere in the globe. Barriers to entry in many industries have fallen drastically or can change very quickly. But even more significant is how the consumer environment has changed. Both businesses and individuals have never before been subjected to the torrent of marketing messages that they currently receive through social media, sophisticated marketing communications and direct marketing techniques. However, psychological studies repeatedly show that consumers attend to very little of this information and that too much choice simply paralyzes decision making. An unambiguous, powerful statement of what you stand for has never been more important.

FORMS OF CUSTOMER VALUE

In competitive industries, businesses win in different ways. In the early 1990s, Ryanair was a small Irish airline on the verge of bankruptcy. After staring into the abyss, the company decided its only option was to take the Southwest Airlines low cost model and drive it even harder in the European market. Twenty years on, it is the second biggest airline in Europe and despite its low price strategy, by far the most consistently profitable firm in an industry renowned for its cyclical profitability. As recently as the late 1990s, competitors in the global vodka industry conducted business as usual competing in the same market segments with brand extensions, price promotions and sometimes clever advertising particularly by the likes of Absolut. It took an entrepreneur from outside the sector, Sidney Frank to recognize that there may be an opportunity in super-premium vodkas in the same way that vintage brandies and whiskies sell so successfully. Without either a vodka distilling plant or a background in the industry he set about building the Grey Goose brand. With its French connections, clever marketing and premium pricing, the product took off and Frank exited the business within eight years for US$2billion while all the incumbents rushed to an increasingly crowded market with their own super-premium offerings.

One of the biggest challenges most businesses have is sorting out what their unique value proposition should be. The competitive dynamics in every industry look different and from time to time different factors are favored. This is particularly true in the case of technology businesses – witness the speed with which Nokia's lead was eroded by smartphone manufacturers, for example. However a careful analysis indicates that there are just four key value positions and these are illustrated in Figure 8.1 below. These are the four primary forms of customer value and firms need to establish a position of strength on one of these dimensions.

Figure 8.1: The Customer Value Quadrant

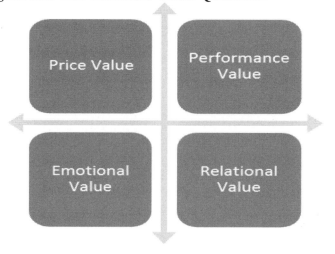

Price Value
Price value has always been and remains a compelling value proposition. You are essentially saying to your customers that you offer you the best price that can be obtained in the market. This is the message that Ryanair gives, that Aldi and Lidl give, that IKEA gives and that many Chinese companies and private label retailers successfully give. It is not about temporary price reductions or even a focus on the discount segment of the market. It is a strategy that makes price the key competitive variable in the industry. Are all these dimensions that competitors talk about really that important if the price is right? Low cost airlines, for example, have been very successful in attracting business customers and in shifting the conversation to a focus on price.

This kind of price leadership means that cost control becomes a key to success. Firms must have the flexibility to adjust major elements of their cost bases. By constantly looking to take cost out of the business system and by flexibly adjusting prices to coincide with demand, low price competitors can generate healthy margins. But it is a constant battle. Low fares airlines have been hurt by rising oil prices that they cannot control and have had to look at ever more ingenious ways of extracting revenue from their customers in order to maintain margins.

Performance Value
Performance value is concerned with offering some form of functionality that is superior to that currently available in the industry. For example, Dyson Ltd revolutionized the staid world of vacuum cleaning with an invention that dispensed with the need for vacuum bags. This innovation catapulted the firm into a leadership position in a multimillion euro industry that had been dominated by industrial giants like Electrolux. In the apparel sector, Zara eschewed the low cost approach of rivals who had garments manufactured in South East Asia in preference for a network of local producers that enabled it to offer range changes every two weeks compared with an industry norm of up to six months. As a result the company's growth has been meteoric. Roxio's distinctive and easy to play games have had a similarly dramatic rise in the rapidly growing app sector.

Historically, performance value was the main basis for competition as firms sought to differentiate products through incremental or major innovation. Winning through performance value is much harder now. Products can be reverse engineered very quickly and patent protection circumvented relatively easily. In many industries, product innovation is relatively mature – for example, in the case of motor cars, almost all brands are reliable and do the job they are supposed to do very well. Realistically there is relatively little difference between competing products in many industries.

One of the net effects has been that margins accruing to firms competing on the basis of performance value have been severely eroded. For example, despite the massive global demand for flat screen televisions, a business which was worth an estimated

US$225billion in 2011, accumulated losses for the makers of LCD screens had reached US$13 billion in the seven years to 2010. Included among the loss making firms are stellar names such as Samsung, Sony and LG. Even the very high margin Apple iPhone has yielded relatively little profit for the Chinese manufacturers that make the components which go into it.

Emotional Value

In a world where the actual differences between competing products diminish, the difference often ends up being in the mind of the consumer. The popular field of behavioral economics appears to be finally putting to bed the idea that the consumer is rational – that is, that she can evaluate all the available alternatives and compute the optimal choices to make. In contrast, decision making both inside and outside the office is characterized by biases, short-cuts and intuitions. It is in this murky world of the subconscious that emotional value resides.

Take for example, Coca Cola. It is one of the world's best known brands and has been frequently rated the most valuable brand in the world over the years. It has seen off many powerful pretenders such as Virgin Cola, Red Bull Cola, retailer brands and most recently Lucozade Energy Cola. Yet it is rarely the preferred brand in taste tests and even fell victim to this rational argument itself in 1985 with the launch of New Coke. It is its associations with youth, fun, happiness and good times built up over years of creative marketing that enables it to remain number one. This even allows it to have two sub-brands, Diet Coke and Coke Zero that are perceived entirely differently even though they are virtually the same drink. Emotional value dominates in the world of consumer goods but it does not stop there. While there are some controls in place and processes that must be followed, business decision making is not free from biases and intuitions either. Managers (and politicians) will often select a consulting firm or supplier because they are perceived to be the best in the business. IBM even made a positioning statement out of this by claiming in their advertising that 'no one ever got fired for recommending IBM!'

Relational Value

Many of the advocates of emotional value recommend trying to push it one more level to that of relational value. This is where a true relationship is formed between a vendor and a customer – where they know each other well, understand each other's needs and co-create value. Customers move up the 'ladder of loyalty' to become supporters, advocates and partners of the business.

Commercial organizations regularly look at sports brands like the All Blacks, Barcelona FC and the Boston Red Sox and yearn for their level of loyalty that endures even though the current team may not be performing well at any given point. Some organizations could claim to have achieved this from time to time – Harley Davidson, Apple, Hollister and others spring to mind. But there is no doubt that the best opportunities to deliver relational value exist in the service and business to business sectors.

Think of the type of relationship that you can build with your doctor, your favorite restaurant or your tax advisor! There is a high level of mutual knowledge, of interaction and of customization. This is what ties two entities together in a business relationship that endures over time. Organizations that are renowned for their service excellence such as Singapore Airlines or the Ritz Carlton generate this type of value.

Other firms try to use technology to build relationships on a global scale such as Tesco with its unique ability to interrogate Club Card data or Amazon with its tracking of buying habits. But winning with relational value is even more demanding than the significant successes that these firms have achieved.

AIM TO BE A VALUE LEADER

The very significant challenge to any business in a competitive industry is to become a value leader on one of the four dimensions outlined above. It is insufficient to simply be good on these dimensions, a firm has to become an industry leader on one otherwise it will not stand out from the crowd. Equally it is ineffective to try to play on multiple dimensions offering price value to price conscious customers and performance value to other customers. Multiple messages, half-hearted messages or constantly changing messages are too confusing and will simply get lost in the ambient noise. Clear, consistent, simple, even blunt messages are increasingly necessary to cut through the clutter. For example, there is no confusion about what the Ryanair value proposition is. It is relentlessly conveyed through its controversial advertising, the very frequent and well-publicized utterings of its senior management and the actual flying experience with the airline itself. It is a message that is understood by management, employees and customers which means that everyone is on the same page strategically!

At the same time, becoming a value leader on one dimension does not mean that the other three quadrants can be ignored. Ryanair would not be very successful if its planes could not do the performance job of transporting passengers effectively. Many observers still wait for one of the low cost carriers to have a major accident to see whether customers will begin to doubt the performance value dimension. In competitive industries being competent of the different dimensions is essential. For example, one of the biggest criticisms of emotional value oriented firms is that they are attempting to sell 'all sizzle and no steak'. There is no point in attempting to build an emotional proposition if your products or services cannot at least do the job as competently as the competition.

Red Bull must give a drinker an energy boost – it simply cannot be all in the mind. BP's very expensive 'beyond petroleum' branding campaign was quickly forgotten after it was involved in a disastrous oil spill in the Gulf of Mexico. In short, firms need to be strong on all dimensions while aiming to be outstanding on one.

CONCLUSION

There are many reasons why firms may want to make customer value leadership a priority and probably one main reason why so many are unwilling to do so. Let us examine the case for initially. Customer value leadership is associated with sustainable success.

This article has identified many firms, mainly large but some small that deliver high levels of customer value with significant medium term performance benefits that are unrelated to economic cycles. There are many more that could be included.

Second, a focus on customer value leadership keeps company strategy firmly anchored in the marketplace. This is critically important. For far too many organizations, strategy is an internal matter with a focus on R&D, innovation, structural change, growth through consolidation or acquisition and so on. This type of inside-out thinking is very risky because market changes often make it irrelevant. Even when the change can be seen coming down the line such as in the case of the music industry or in firms like Kodak, management still pushed on with internally-focused initiatives that were ultimately ineffective.

And finally, the pursuit of customer value leadership can be a highly motivating goal for an organization's workforce. Many of the traditional motivators for employees such as job longevity, pension rights and security are long gone. At the same time there is an expectation of almost 24/7 availability and involvement with work. To keep employees motivated in this environment requires the creation of an almost missionary zeal around something worth striving for. That level of genuine employee effort is one of the few sustainable competitive advantages left for business because it is so hard to create and replicate.

So why would firms not be willing to make customer value leadership the core focus of their strategy? In short, because it is very difficult, for some people the idea is too nebulous. Sales and profit targets or market share leadership are things that can be measured and seen but customer value leadership is not so clear though there are many indicative measures for each of the four forms of value outlined above. Other managers may see the idea as too complex. What does performance value or emotional value actually mean in my industry? This takes us into the realm of understanding what the market wants – a notoriously difficult thing to accurately gauge despite the range of research tools available.

And finally customer value leadership requires relentless effort.

This is no quick fix or something than can be achieved with a short CEO tenure. Instead it is a return to Drucker's classic notion that businesses have just one purpose, namely, to create and keep customers. All the rest are spinoffs. The focus is not on quarterly numbers but on a strategic goal that is not derailed even when the short term returns are not what stakeholders would like.

In a bid to cut through the television advertising clutter, Honda recently decided to run a well-publicized live advert that involved filming a group of sky divers as they descended in the air and spelled out the word 'Honda'. Their slogan for the campaign was 'difficult is worth doing'. The same could be said for the pursuit of customer value leadership.

About the Author:*An award winning international researcher and teacher, John Fahy is Professor of Marketing at the University of Limerick. He has a distinguished track record in the fields of marketing resources, marketing capabilities, and business strategy.*

Other current research interests include customer value, evolutionary perspectives on marketing and strategic decision making and his popular blog on these issues at www.johnfahy.net .

His articles on marketing and strategy that have been published in: **JOURNAL OF MARKETING, JOURNAL OF INTERNATIONAL BUSINESS STUDIES, JOURNAL OF BUSINESS RESEARCH, JOURNAL OF MARKETING MANAGEMENT, EUROPEAN JOURNAL OF MARKETING, INTERNATIONAL BUSINESS REVIEW and SLOAN MANAGEMENT REVIEW.** *John is the author of several award winning business case studies and of two books including the best-selling **Foundations of Marketing** co-written with David Jobber.*

Professor Fahy holds a Master's Degree from Texas A&M University, a Doctorate from Trinity College, and serves on the Executive Committee of the European Academy of Marketing.

9. The Indirect Sales Channel by *Sharmila Wijeyakumar*

EXECUTIVE SUMMARY

There is the method of how to be strategically placed for the indirect sales channel and what channel partners are looking for. Flowing with the current wave and why it is the wave of the future for software companies to expand globally. What is cloud and how can this be part of the vendor's business model. Is there a clear direction as to how to work with cloud or is it just based on a theory that is unproven.

INTRODUCTION

Sales & Marketing for The Indirect Sales Channel

Vendors, Value added Resellers & Systems integrators have long been entwined in relationships for mutual benefit. Direct vs. indirect it is a constant argument in the software industry particularly for start-up companies. As an independent consultant I often get start-up asking me how to globalize and my answer is always grow your channel base. This is inevitably when I have to explain why a direct sales force is not the right choice.

Over my 15 years working in software I have found that all start-ups are always cash strapped with big expansion plans. Now software always needs support in local languages and local time zones so it is rare that cash strapped start-ups can manage to scale to this level fast even if they have Venture Capital funding. Another classic start up problem is the lack of local market knowledge including cultural knowledge that makes all the difference in the globalization process. This is where a channel approach can help.

Why an Indirect Sales Channel?

An indirect approach allows small software start-ups to:-

- Avoid the cost of hiring & churn in a direct sales force – The hiring , firing and normal turnover of a sales team is a very expensive situation for a software start-up

- Plan for a localized globalization approach country by country – The skills of a local approach mean that you overcome the normal contractual issues in a country by using a reseller channel and avoid the high costs of an office in every country

- Leverage the relationships the local partner has in their home country – Partners always have flagship customers to whom they are a trusted adviser this status allows them to test new ideas as long as they meet the needs of the business

- Improve customer service deliver in local language – Customers like to be managed locally & in their own language giving them this option will always improve emergence into a new geography

- Provide support in local time zones – You can't be awake 24/7 and nor can your team so local partners can help you implement a follow the sun approach to support

- Manage marketing programs on a local level – Local partners will often know what marketing works best where in the USA newspaper ads will not likely deliver an audience to a software event in Africa this just may be the right medium.

What do Channel Partners Really want?

No matter which way you look at it an indirect approach for a software start-up is always the way to market. It saves money, reduces risk and increases market penetration while improving support. I am a firm believer that the only way to market for a software start-up looking to globalize is via an indirect channel and you will know that I feel the Vendor has many benefits for going this route; but what about the channel partner the WITFM factor has to come into play. Business is after all a place for win-win so how do vendors & their channel strike a balance?

What they want most of all is obvious – to make money! But a few other factors apply.

- To have transparency both in pipeline (vendors want this too), roadmap & internal policy – nothing scares a channel as much as change that is unplanned and not well managed.

- To have a direct human who is dedicated to their account – a place from which everything else is coordinated.

- The ability to access support when needed – often a direct line to engineering make a remarkable difference in the comfort level of a partner

- To have no competition from the vendor – the age old Direct vs Indirect saga of many a multinational (and some smaller OS BI vendors who shall remain nameless...)

- To know that the vendor can be trusted not to pass over leads provided by 1 partner to another one – this is tricky as it relies on people but good process always helps

- To have a product that works and does what it says on the box. – this may seem obvious but many a zealous marketing department has left many a partner with a mess to clean up post sale.

Dedication of the Vendor to make the channel successful – Partners want to see proved that this vendor backs its partners and values them as part of their sales team providing them with Lead gen opportunities – this one is critical for success

Seems simple but to deliver this well across many countries regions & partner types can make any sales director's head spin. I was once lucky enough to not have built 3 channels on new products from scratch and am now on my 4th as well as been on the other side of the desk working for SI's & resellers and I can honestly say process, process, process!

If a software start-up wants to build a channel for distribution Process is key and if you don't make the fatal mistakes I mentioned above you will be off to a good start.

Partners like Vendors who are invested in the channel and who is more vested than a software start-up with a largely channel based model and reliance on the channel. This is a marriage made in Heaven for both Vendors & partners alike.

"HOW TO' BEST PRACTICES

How Software Vendors can help Channel Partners Cloud strategy?

Today the word Cloud is thrown around regularly and every company in software is trying to decide its unique strategy for cloud. We have multiple differing views, there is a school of thought that says cloud is the way of the future, & a school that says cloud is a passing phase. I am of the school of thought defending cloud as a wave of the future. Between icloud, evernote, dropbox, etc. companies & individuals are migrating in the direction of "wave of the future". Personally, I love the cloud. I like the idea that anywhere, anytime, I can access and use my information and the disaster recovery potential is also very helpful.

- With this in mind, why are there so many channel partners & software vendors suffering from a lack of clear direction on this topic? The main issue seems to be lack of understanding and fear.

- Channel partners are also further confused by the lack of general support from vendors but the vendors are equally confused so are not laying out clear strategies. VAR's are also concerned that if they resell cloud based systems hosted by the vendors they may potentially lose control of their customers. It also causes VAR's problems with commission structures, marketing and infrastructure costs.

- In today's economic downturn it only makes sense that companies want to implement solutions which have a small investment and are easy to implement, so it should come as no surprise that cloud is growing in popularity. Now let's leave aside some of the issues cloud raises and it does raise reasonable concerns around security of data, ownership of data and confidentiality. But even in the face of these it provides end users with access anywhere, anytime and with the climate needed to make a sale changing and sales cycles growing in length cloud can offer faster ROI's.

- This said there are 2 types of customers investing

- Ones looking for competitive advantages

- Those who can no longer wait to make a decision due to contractual pressures or business needs

- With all this said it seems strange that while customers are looking for fresh new approaches channel partners and many Vendors are paralyzed to adopt real strategies for cloud.

So what are channel partners worried about?

- Costs and investment needed to create a real cloud Practice

- Reliability of the cloud

- Scalability of the offerings

- Loss of control over the customer

- How to transform their business model to include cloud offerings

- How to compensate sales people on these new models

- How to market these strategies effectively and not cut into the current customer base revenue streams

- How to handle billing on these

How can Vendors Help?

- Vendors can share with selected partners in the costs of creating infrastructures that are scalable & repeatable to adapt to the needs of a changing market & teach partners how to best adapt to the cloud offerings

- Vendors can deploy strategies to not compete with partners and to provide partners with equal control over customers and decision about those customers

- Vendors must run training sessions to help partners to understand all possible cloud based revenue models for their product offerings and work with partners to help them to choose the best options for the greatest win-win outcome for all parties involved.

- Vendors should offer whitepapers, videos & other training to assist SME's to compensate their sales force appropriately for the new business models so they are profitable to all

- Vendors need to build repeatable adaptable marketing campaigns to assist channel partners with out of the box marketing messaging & collateral that is easily reused by partners in their local markets along with ways to maintain & grow current customer bases by expanding the reach of the partner with innovative cloud offerings

- Vendors can simplify billing for partners by offering vendor based billing that pays a commission to partners on a monthly or quarterly basis

Obviously this is just the tip of the iceberg on this complex issue and if vendors & partners are to break through the stronghold holding them back communication & collaboration is the only way forward.

How can Channel Partners sell more Cloud Based Services?

If you asked 100 people you would get 100 different answers about what the cloud is. The silver lining in this is that it means you can define your cloud strategy so it personally fits your business. The cloud is an opportunity for VAR's and one that should be embraced particularly in these trying economic times. The ability to reduce the entry barrier costs and build a recurring revenue stream is well worth the effort.

There are 3 main cloud type business models:

1. IAAS – Infrastructure as a service

2. PAAS – Platform as a Service

3. SAAS – Software as a service

The best example I can give is of IAAS AMAZON you basically rent space from them but you have to manage it entirely. Examples of PAAS is Entando or Microsoft Azure where solution providers can create vertical applications or deliver specialized services with increased speed due to infrastructure to build on being in place from the vendor. A SAAS example could be Entando's Sales Analytics Module which is a part of their overall offering but out of the box ready to deploy and available in the cloud, other famous examples include Microsoft office 365, or Google apps.

It is usually PAAS or SAAS that is most interesting to the VAR community. With platforms like Azure & Entando partners can design bespoke verbalized solutions and monetize them if they choose in somewhat of a cloud based OEM type model and most software vendors with these types of platforms have special partner programs to assist VARS who wish to go this route. It is however the SAAS model that attracts the most attention from VARS.

Most VAR's have realized that margins paid by vendors on the resale of SAAS solutions are not going to make them rich but will over time create a nice renewable revenue stream; however, this is not the only revenue creation model for VAR's. The best way to make money from a SAAS sale is to wrap value added services around the SAAS provided by the vendor. Now VAR's have been doing this for years in the traditional software market so it begs the question for me why all the hysteria around doing it for cloud based offerings?

Fear! Fear is the VAR's greatest enemy, VAR's build businesses on added value to a vendors offering as such VAR's need to approach the market with agility and be able to adapt to changing market conditions & changing Vendor conditions. With this in mind there is no place for fear. Instead consider all the normal types of value added services you provide and customize them for cloud.

Types of Services may include:
- Deployment
- Migration
- Support
- Off-site back up

- Disaster recovery

These are not new to a VAR they have been providing these with their own "secret sauce" for years, so why adapt?

VARs have to adapt because Customers love the cloud. They love it because:

- The can achieve rapid deployment – often even the same day

- They can minimize the start-up costs and in today's economic times this makes sense.

- Less CAPEX more OPEX – they can lower capital expenditure and increase operational expenditure which often times makes the office of finance happier. No depreciation to calculate and OPEX is usually fully tax deductible.

- Low management overheads – great for small businesses or those without an IT department.

Why should a VAR embrace it?
- Can provide recurring revenue stream

- Can shorten sales cycles due to reduced start – up costs

- Can allow for departmental solutions without needing to go via IT or Procurement

- If you don't offer it you will start losing deals to VAR's that do

VAR's will have to continue to be agile and able to continue to be the trusted advisor your customer's needs.

CONCLUSION

The selling indirectly requires persistence & relationship management. Vendors and channel partners need to continue to work hard at relationships and make sure the communication is consistent & collaborative if success is to be a win-win combination.

This collaboration will instill a good working relationship between the vendors and the partners. There will be a clear understanding of the fears and concerns from both sides. A Channel provides a clear picture of Cloud and its cost, reliability, scalability etc. Channel Partners working with vendors will educate the vendors on how not lose the control of customers and how to cloud can be part of the business model. Understanding that no way is 100% sure, but with good communication and leadership from VAR's the customer is able to produce more effectively which in turn benefits everyone.

REFERENCES

Blog - swijeyakumar.wordpress.com

About the Author: Sharmila's (Sam), Vice President of Sales and Marketing for Entando, brings her professional knowledge in Enterprise software emerging International Markets to companies like Microsoft, ICS, & TAH.

As the Director of Channel for EMEA and APAC at Pentaho, she was recognized as one of the Top 100 most powerful women in the Channel by CRN magazine in 2011 for leading the drive to accomplish 286% growth in EMEA. She repeated this honor in 2012 for design & deployment of a new channel program at Entando. Cambridge Institute inducted her as a Lifetime member in the Who's Who of Women in IT.

Sharmila has extensive direct & indirect sales skills and is best known for her ability to emerge software products into new markets. She routinely launches successful software, both proprietary & open source into North America, Europe, the Middle East, Africa and Asia Pacific. A strong believer in a channel philosophy for software distribution especially in emerging markets, she is currently working to reinvent and commoditize the portal market with Entando.

Sharmila holds a Masters of Business Administration and Bachelor of Science in Business Administration from Indiana University-Purdue University at Fort Wayne.

10. How to Make Social Media Work for Your Business by *Zara Sheerin*

EXECUTIVE SUMMARY

Social media has been the buzzword of the last number of years, we've all heard about it, many companies are using it but are you using it to your advantage? This paper will focus on the evolution of social media as a marketing channel, why it's gained such prominence, why it's so important, what you can do to start making waves online, what works and some common pitfalls.

This paper is for anyone who has a web presence and for anyone who doesn't. Whether you are a VP of a multinational or run a startup business - it's vital that you understand the power of social media and how it can help you reach existing and potential customers.

INTRODUCTION

Social media is nothing new, we're still having the same conversations we've always had - except now as a business you have the opportunity to be part of that conversation. And of course there's a right way and a wrong way to do that.

The evolution of online marketing:
Online marketing was one of the few sectors to experience growth as the global recession hit - not in spite of it, but because of it. Suddenly, even big brands no longer had huge budgets to spend producing TV ads, and so they began to 'dip their toes in the water' with online media. Return on investment on a marketing budget and cost per acquisition became even more pertinent, and so with online marketing's innate measurability - the focus began to shift towards this medium. Blanket advertising to the masses was no longer the best approach to advertising, targeted and specific messaging that reached key audiences with the appropriate messages, coupled with

the cost effectiveness of the medium, made online marketing a no-brainer for those in-tune.

Figure 1, below, shows the huge growth in online advertising spend in Ireland, while all other mediums are in sharp decline, this really underpins the significance of online as a marketing channel. An IAB PwC Online Adspend Study values the Irish online market at €110m, which represents a 12.2% increase in ad spend year-on-year. Bartley O'Connor, Advisory Consultant at PwC notes that "the growth in the Irish online audience and in their time spent consuming online media while other media are experiencing fragmenting audiences underlines the phenomenon of online's growing share of media budgets".

Figure 10.1: Comparative advertising spend in Ireland

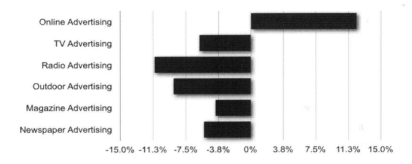

Some key drivers for this growth include the increase in broadband penetration and a much higher time spent online - as a result of online video, streamed TV & films and of course social media. The average time spent online each week has increased from 13 hours to 19 hours year-on-year.

Online marketing today:
Fast forward to 2012, and online has increasingly become the medium of choice not just for big brands but for small to medium sized companies as well. But with so many companies vying for a

customer's attention, marketers have had to find innovative new ways to achieve the all-important 'cut-through'.

To really engage through social media marketers need to draw the user in. It's not a case of 'if you build it they will come', to quote the 1980's Kevin Costner movie! To achieve visibility on the web a brand must stand out, drawing their target audience in through incentives - engaging and entertaining the prospective customer. People do not like being sold to. It's about "telling" rather than "selling", it's vitally important to encourage a two-way dialogue with consumers - and that is a fundamental shift in the way we advertise. People follow brands that are current, entertaining, informative, and above all, one's that provide value. It's important to reward visitors on a brands social media presence - this can be done through entertaining content, coupon codes, special offers, or fan-only content. This sort of instant payoff will help earn their trust and loyalty. Avoid sales heavy social campaigns, selling, pushing and pitching too much doesn't give your community anything of value, use the Pareto 80/20 rule, eighty percent content, twenty percent sales.

From hairdressing salons and hotels to multinationals and SME's, a huge proportion of companies have become aware of the importance of social media and are incorporating it into their marketing mix. It's hard to turn on the TV or pick up a local paper without seeing the 'follow us' call to action from companies beckoning you to like them on Facebook or follow them on twitter. However, it's about using social media as a platform (figure 2) for all other mediums to feed through to, having a 'Find us on Facebook' call to action on every ad is not enough - businesses need to have a strategy in place to really leverage social media as a channel. It has to be about engaging people and offering them a payback through interesting content, competition prizes and offers. In short, being visible online. Make online a destination - make it serve as a platform for all other communications to feed into.

Figure 10.2: Don't forget about traditional mediums -

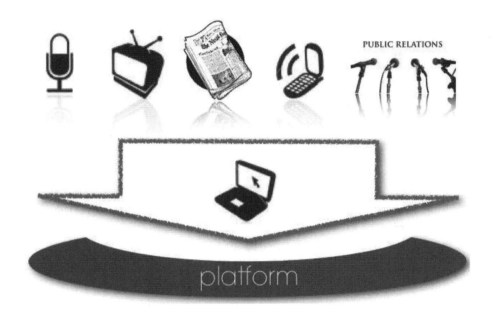

Is Your Brand Visible Online?

Every minute of every day, more than a half-billion members of Facebook collectively create almost 1 million photos, wall posts, status updates, and other bits of content. Twitter looks tame by comparison - the network sees more than 125,000 tweets a minute. YouTube receives more than 48 hours of video per minute. If you watched video every minute of your life, you'd get through 10 days' worth of YouTube uploads. This shows the level of competition online, to achieve visibility on the social web, a brand needs to leave breadcrumbs and footprints in all the right places to draw people to you. It's important to plan a brands social media strategy, it's about creating a buzz to draw the target audience in organically, to be seen by the right people at the right time - combining strategic visibility with excellent customer service results in a community that can't help but rave about your company.

The New York Times interviewed students in NYU a couple of years ago, to garner information on their media consumption. They asked students what papers they bought, what radio stations they listened to, one young man simply responded "If the news is important enough, it will find me" - what a powerful statement, and from a company's point of view, if your latest tweet or update isn't 'newsworthy' enough to your audience, it quite simply will not be seen.

A brand must ensure that they are contributing quality information and building connections naturally, they need to be insightful, engaging, and provocative when creating a dialogue. Invoke emotions: i.e. for a charity that emotion may be guilt, for a festival it may be excitement. If facilitated, consumers can become a company's 'brand advocates' - personally producing content for them, becoming part of their campaign and spreading their brand message to their network.

The 'Active' Consumer: We have moved from being a passive consumer to an active consumer, we're now producing content as part of campaigns that seek user generated content, we participate in campaigns online if we find them compelling enough, we're part of the multiplier effect - if we see something we like online we 'like', 'share' or 'retweet' - spreading the message to our own network, and we're all a part of various different communities - the task for the marketer or brand owner is to tap in to the relevant community, elicit a reaction from the consumer by getting them to produce content, participate in the campaign and spread the message virally. Figure 3 demonstrates this.

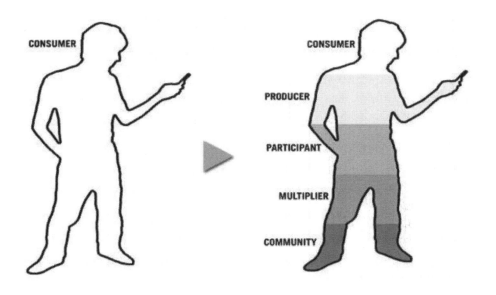

Figure 10.3: The Changing Consumer

Brand Ambassadors: A brand is no longer what a company says about its product, it's what a friend tells a friend. If a brand can get the user to engage, share and personalize – they become their brand ambassadors. Think of the now infamous T-Mobile YouTube ads (youtube.com/lifesforsharing), in a series of very public stunts from the Liverpool Street and Heathrow airport flash mobs, to the parking ticket videos, T-Mobile managed to live their brand mantra 'Life is for Sharing' by creating some of the most sharable, humorous, feel-good content online. These stunts led to people videoing the events as they happened and spreading them online and through their phones, most of these videos have between 20 and 35 million YouTube views, I compel you not to 'laugh out loud' or even shed a tear watching them! T-Mobile succeeded in making 'Life is for Sharing' far more than just a tagline, it is the embodiment of everything their company ethos represents.

Give Fans a Reason to Visit You:
The corner stone of any successful social strategy is to give back to your fan base. If you don't give fans free things, discounts, coupons, competitions, games – or engage them in any way, they're not going to engage with you. Mint Digital has been leading the social media strategy for the Galway Shopping Centre and their five sister centers throughout the country to boost their online presence and avail of the viral reach Facebook has to offer. The Valentine's quiz 'Share the Love' offers customers the chance to win a host of prizes - the content is fresh, funny and on-brand so the payoff is entertaining content coupled with a large number of prizes, incentivizing entries. This is a spin off from the Christmas campaign 'Pass the Parcel' which led to a 470% increase in their fan base.

Mint Digital also worked on a hugely successful Facebook campaign for the Salthill Hotel. The Salthill Hotel was looking to raise brand awareness and increase bookings by using Facebook as a promotional tool. Tapping into the old Galway tradition of 'kicking the wall' at the prom in Blackrock, the Facebook App invited users to 'Pic the Wall' by adding their profile picture to this virtual version of the wall. Daily prizes were given away to drive people to the fan page and to encourage them to take part and discuss the competition. Hits to the Salthill Hotel website increased by 55% and referrals from Facebook to the site jumped up 6 places, most importantly; there was an incredibly high increase in online sales as a direct result of the campaign.

Figure 10.4: Mint's approach to client campaigns

How to make Social Media work for you:

- Offer value - either through engaging content, previews, coupons, prizes or offers. Recruit through games and daily prizes.

- Achieve visibility - stand out through engaging campaigns, use popular references - make sure your campaign resonates.

- Be conversational - create a tone of voice that cuts through and engages. It should be a dialogue.

- Loyalty - build a loyal customer base to leverage organic spread.

- Resource - be ready to respond to your customers and encourage them to talk about your brand.

- Commitment - be ready to make a commitment beyond a campaign.

- Integration - know how any other marcomm strategies will integrate with your social media campaign. Are there other assets (tools and content) can you leverage?
- Use images and videos - The rise of visual storytelling as a means of spreading a marketing message has been immense. Image-based platforms like, pinterest, instagram and slide share have already made a strong statement about how visual content can impact business results, as has Facebook Timeline. Images are some of the most popular pieces of content shared by brands and can help reach the masses spreading your brand message to a much wider audience.
- Measurability - think about how you will measure success.

Some Common Pitfalls to avoid:

- ✘ Posting too frequently. The recommended number of posts for brands is about 1 – 2 posts per day
- ✘ Not engaging with people in comments. Don't forget that you have to engage with your fans and respond to them – make sure you reply to people when they have questions.
- ✘ Arguing with your fans. If you have an angry fan, answer unemotionally and drive the conversation elsewhere.
- ✘ Deleting negative comments. Never delete negative comments. Never, almost never... 99.99% never!
- ✘ Running competitions against the sites rules. Don't announce winners solely over Facebook, ensure you have adequate terms and conditions, and a data policy
- ✘ Not using applications/tabs. The best thing about Facebook is that you can create a campaign that will drive and boost your community organically.
- ✘ Sending your fans to your site only. Sending fans to your site is not the best way of keeping your community really active and sharing. Communities love videos and pictures, but if you just send them links to your page only, that won't do the trick (unless it's really relevant content), but always make sure to mix the content.

✘   Not using Facebook landing tabs. Landing tabs are a very important part of your Facebook page, and can make your page grow 40% faster.

CONCLUSION

Think about your target audience, who are they, where are they, what do they want to hear. Then devise your communications strategy - ensure you have a content plan outlining your company's tone of voice, content ideas to maximize the potential for user generated content. Create opportunities to recruit organically through engaging content. Think about what value means to your fans, create a competition to achieve viral reach. When a robust fan base has been achieved you then have a platform to communicate regularly to fans with little media cost.

REFERENCES

Figure 1: IAB Pricewaterhouse Coopers Online Adspend Survey 2009-2010

Time spent online: increased from 13.2 (ComReg) in 2009 to 19.1 hours per week in 2010 (Red C).

Shel Isreal: Author of Twitterville (2009);'It's about "telling" rather than "selling"'

About the Author:
Zara Sheerin graduated from NUIG (National University of Ireland Galway), with a BA (Hons) in Public and Social Policy, with a focus on Law and Economics. She then went on to Post Graduate studies in Business and Marketing in (Dublin Business School), obtaining a first class honors for her thesis on the topic of Consumer Buyer Behavior.

Zara established Mint Digital Marketing in March 2011 after years of working in cutting edge digital agencies in Dublin and London, including Harvest Digital, Cawley Nea/TBWA and Bluecube Interactive. Zara led the digital strategy for worldwide brands such as Audi, Jameson, Etihad Airways and Ulster Bank, as well as great Irish national brands like ESB, Meteor and Change.ie.

Mint is a full service digital marketing agency based in Galway - with a specific focus on developing social media campaigns that deliver real engagement and tangible results as well as email marketing strategies, web design & development, search marketing and strategic planning.

11. Your Marketing and Sales Strategy by *Blaise Brosnan*

INTRODUCTION

You are in a commercial business and its foundation is based on ensuring that your revenues are consistently greater than your total costs, so that you can get an acceptable return on your investment (ROI). Revenue represents the combination of having enough customers buying from you but at acceptable margins. The corner stone of this formula is to optimize your sales. Your marketing strategy will facilitate this.

Process

Developing a marketing strategy is vital for any business. Without one, your efforts to attract customers are likely to be haphazard and inefficient. Marketing is a communication process of positively influencing potential and existing customers in your favor. Creating a marketing strategy will help you identify potential customers and target them with appropriate products or services. Using the correct sales techniques will help you turn interest in your product or service into customer orders and follow-on retained profits. As your trading environment is constantly changing, your strategy and "offering" to your targeted market needs to be in tune with these changes.

Your big issue is how to inform your target market that you exist and then generate their necessary response.

BUILDING THE WINNING STRATEGY

Matching: Knowing and understanding your customer's <u>needs and wants</u> is at the center of every successful business. You have to better understand <u>who</u> your target market is, what their "pain" is and the symptoms around this pain. You must then present your solution / proposition in such a way that they can automatically link your solution with their pain. This matching is the critical cornerstone of good marketing.

Every business needs a reason for their customers to buy from them and not from their competitors. This is called its Unique Sales Proposition (USP). It's important to understand that it's your customers and potential customers who decide whether your USP is relevant to them or not. Your marketing tactics aims to influence these decisions in your favour. Remember - if your competitors are perceived to be doing the same as you, your USP isn't unique any more. Strong sales are driven by emphasizing the benefits that your product or service brings to your customers. If you know the challenges they face, it's much easier to offer them appropriate solutions.

Market Research: *The critical issue influencing which marketing / selling tactics to use is to better understand whether your "offering" should be pitched as a solution to a basic <u>need</u> or <u>nice-to-have want</u> in your targeted customers head.*

When creating your marketing strategy, you need to understand your target market and its trends - ie the specific group of consumers you will be aiming your products or services at. These are the customers who are most likely to buy from you, and who will make your business successful. You should build your Business Model on what the market is telling you. You get back this information from the market via Market Research (MR).

You need to be clear what your marketing objectives are in different time zones. Are you looking to increase your Brand awareness or are you looking for a direct sales response. Your marketing tactics need to reflect these objectives. There are many techniques and tactics you can use to inform and influence the purchasing decisions of your target market. Clarity re the following issues will help you to fine-tune your tactics.

1. Who are they?
2. What do they do?
3. Why do they buy your type of "offering"
4. When and where do they buy?
5. Trends on how they buy?
6. Their Net-worth.
7. What they think about your Brand.
8. Other similar type "offering" they buy and from whom.
9. Price-points.

With this clarity of market information you must then organize your "offering" to more precisely reflect the mood of this targeted market better than your competitors, as perceived by these existing and potential customers. Satisfied customers will ultimately make your rich.

Listed here are the normal steps to be taken when you are doing market research.

1. **Define your targeted area of interest.**
2. **Define your Market Research objectives.**
   a. **What are you trying to find out?**
   b. **A combination of quantitative and qualitative type information on.**
      i. **Competitors.**
      ii. **Trends.**
      iii. **The parameters of your interested niches.**
      iv. **Preferred features and benefits for the various identified niches.**
      v. **Evolving customer's preferences.**
      vi. **Others.**
      vii. **?????**
3. **Decide how best to get this information.**
   a. **What tactics are you going to use.**
4. **Secondary Research.**
   a. **What relevant information / Data is already published.**
      i. **What are the identified opportunities coming across from this research?**
5. **Primary Research in order to test some of the assumptions re the opportunities identified from the Secondary Research.**
   a. **Focused groups.**
   b. **Surveys.**
      i. **Postal.**
      ii. **Phone.**
      iii. **Questionnaires.**
      iv. **Observations.**

Good Market Research will give you a good "feel" for what the market wants and more importantly what it DEMANDS.

The market is made up of a series of niches. From your Market Research you will have identified the niche(s) with the most potential for your "offering". This segmentation can be based on such relevant criteria as.

1. Geography.
2. Demographics.
3. Age groups.
4. Net Worth / spending power.
5. Others.

You need to know your core target markets characteristics', so that you can be more precise in pitching your marketing message. *It's the one bullet rather than the scatter gun approach.* You will of course gain some business on either side of this defined niche.

> Now that you know your target niches and their preferences, you can pitch your marketing message accordingly. You do this under two headings.

1. Benefits.
    a. Benefits represent 80% of why they buy.
    b. What "issue" does your target customer have?
    c. What BENEFIT does your proposition have to address this issue?
2. Features.
    a. Features represent 20% of why they buy.
    b. The features are the packages your BENEFITS are wrapped in.

Market positioning and Branding: With your enhanced reading of your targeted markets dynamics, you are now fit to decide your marketing strategy. The critical decision here is where you decide to position your "offering" on the market. Are you going to operate at the premium or the commodity end of the spectrum or at what point between these two extremes.

All the elements of your marketing mix must be appropriate for this agreed market positioning. This is really articulated by your Branding and all its associated perceptions and understandings.

Your Brand represents the DNA of your business. It is the equivalent of your own personal name. When someone mentions your personal name, what sort of thoughts click into their head about you. People have put their lives at risk in order to defend their good name.

Your business BRAND is the same. You're Logo and Brand name needs to symbolize in your potential customers mind what you are about and the positive implications for them. Be your brand, live your brand by ensuring that your company truly expresses the brand identity you've established. Branding makes it easier for potential customers to make their buying decisions. When they see your brand, their minds will register a particular reaction based on their previous experiences and influencers. If it has been a good experience, they will feel more confident parting with their money.

You must constantly deliver your promise and if you do that you will build brand loyalty. This will lead to repeat and referred business. This is your wealth creation formula. You must have the same mind-set in building and consistently defending your business Brand as you would your personal name.

Your BRAND is the glue that keeps all your marketing tactics together. By putting your targeted customer at the CENTRE, then your build your Business model to more precisely satisfy them than your competitor down the road. They will thank you via their unconscious consistent purchasing. Branding ensures that your "offering" is less price sensitive and provides you with the opportunity for greater margins and follow on wealth building.

You can use the following communication channels to get your Branding message out to the targeted market niche(s).

1. Direct mail.
2. Trade shows.
3. PR.
4. Print media advertising.
5. Outdoor advertising.

6. Radio / TV.
7. Search engine optimization.
8. Pay per click.
9. Social media.
10. Networking.
11. Telesales.
12. Direct selling.
13. Sponsorship.
14. Promotions.
15. Merchandising.
16. Guerrilla marketing.

You need to decide the budget and then what tactic or combination of these "tools" you are going to use to effectively speak with your target niche(s). Lay out your marketing plan as a project sheet, showing who is going to do what where and when and within which budget.

You need to be smart in optimising this marketing budget in order to achieve your targeted ROI.

The five P's of marketing are.

1. Product.
2. Place.
3. Promotion.
4. Price.
5. People.

You have to develop an integrated <u>Action Plan</u> to optimise each of these "pillars" so as to facilitate your ultimate sales objectives.

Marketing in its totality brings and influences your targeted customers to the point of sale.

If your "offering" is small ticket, then your will expect automatic follow-on sales from your marketing interventions. Your processes must make it convenient for your targeted customers to spend their money.

If your "offering" is big ticket, then you have to follow on your marketing interventions with effective face to face selling techniques. I will address just one of these selling techniques in this article. The chosen one is known as suggestion selling.

Suggestion Selling: You can sell more products to your customer aside from the item that they are currently buying. *This is possible through suggestion selling.* Suggestion selling is selling necessary additional goods and services to the customer. It involves selling customers complementary items that will ultimately save them time and money, or makes the original purchase more enjoyable.

Some of you will be naturals in this area. For those who are not natural, you can become very effective salespeople if you model yourself on the following sale tactics.

Timing is very important. Make the original sale and then in the time space between this and the payment, start suggesting complementary items. This intervention by you needs to be perceived by the customer as a desire on your part to help them to have a better experience from their purchase. *In reality it's a mutual experience.*

Support your suggestion with your strongest evidence from the customer's perspective. If you start giving too many reasons you will dilute your argument. Make the suggestion in the form of a question, keep silent and let the customer respond. The first person who breaks the silence will lose. Make sure you keep in charge of the process. Get the customer involved in creating a better solution for them. You need to match their predominant communication / personality type. If the customer is a touchy / feeling type person, then get them to take the item into their hand. Then they will become attached to it and thank you for your concern. *This leads to a repeat customer.* You need to set them up so that they are buying from you rather than you selling to them. You do this by playing to their ego.

If you do this effectively, then you will be able to bank the resultant extra revenue.

CONCLUSION

Your future commercial success depends on your capability of growing your sales at good margins. By adopting and consistently implementing some of the strategies and tactics addressed in this article, you too can enjoy the fruits of your labour.

"The one who adapts his policy to the times prospers, and likewise that the one whose policy clashes with the demands of the times does not" (Niccolo Machiavelli)

About the Author: *During his distinguished tenure as CEO of WFC, Blaise built the business from a humble baseline to become a multi-million business. In 1995, he launched **Management Resource Institute (MRI**-www.mriwex.ie**)**. This business specializes in a range of interrelated services including business consulting, management training and commercial mediation services. His practical understanding of the dynamics of management equips him to make **meaningful interventions** for global clients at various stages of the "life-cycles" of their businesses.*

*In 2008 he launched his first book, **You are the Limiting Factor**, is a management resource book. His second book, **Jack-business lessons from life, life lessons from business** contains "nuggets of wisdom" reflecting our reactions to life issues.*

Blaise holds a Bachelor's Degree in Agricultural Economics from UCD and a Masters in Management

Part Two: Your Business Competitive Advantage

12..Pipelines of creativity are the foundation of continues innovation in company by *Richard Lawler*

EXECUTIVE SUMMARY

This article gives an over view of the book *"Innovation Demystified Tapping into our creative core"* and a sample of some of the best practices and tools contained within the book. The article challenges business owners and management to be more holistic in how they run their operations to ensure that the workforce can develop their own creativity the result of which can be the business reaping the rewards when the creativity is focused into innovation.

The best practices include – removing the illusion of explanatory depth of key operational terms, understanding what influences individual creativity and the basic flow of an innovation pipeline.

BEST PRACTICES TO DEMYSTIFY INNOVATION

Removing the illusion of explanatory depth of key operational terms

The illusion of explanatory depth is a term in physiology used when people think they know what a term means, but are unable to explain it in depth. When a CEO speaks of innovation in reality the majority of the organization is not using the same definition and are often confused by what they are hearing. To solve this each company should adopt a formal definition, which will be published and referenced by all in the organization to ensure comprehension of instructions and statements. Failure to do so is speaking without common reference points and holly open to miss understanding.

The following are suggested definitions of creativity and innovation that your business might consider formally adopting.

"Creativity is the production of novel and useful ideas by an individual or small group of individuals working together. "

"Innovation is an organizational process that begins with a creative idea that is implemented to deliver a new product, service, process, or business model to the market place."

Understanding what influences individual creativity

The book devotes considerable space to the need for the creation of personal creativity plans and creative comfort zone development. It address in a holistic way how diet and exercise can affect your ability to take in new information and process it into new ideas, as well as the impact of the built environment on your creativity and how to address it.

The best practice here is supplying you with fresh information and learning on which and out of which to generate creative ideas. Ask yourself how often do I learn new things, how am I supplying new experience and knowledge to myself on an ongoing basis?

You must plant seeds in a field in order to harvest a crop right? Part of your plan for increasing personal creativity should involve reading of books, at least one every two weeks. It is useful to alternate between books on and around your field of business and others that are random. The Idea being to get exposure to new ideas and ways of thinking that could help you with your own idea generation. Also take a course in creative writing, dancing or public speaking, which will also expose you to new people who will challenge your points of view and help you improve the quality of your ideas.

The flow of an innovation pipeline

Innovation is the result of a chain of events but which events? In general start with a problem statement evolving it until you have really captured the essence of the problem as below. After you have defined your problem statement you focus on generation of ideas, evaluation of ideas and implementation of those ideas.

The problem statement best practice - Let us say you have a problem statement you should take your initial statement and develop it first, try the following:

- Rewrite the original problem in 10 different ways
- Draw a diagram of the problem
- List the causes, not just the symptoms of the problem
- List the minor details and big picture perspective
- Canvass a wide range of views
- Keep asking "why?"
- Change the underlying assumptions of the problem

The result is often better insight into the problem, better understanding of the problem you are trying to solve, you discover you're really trying to solve a different problem and in some cases discover it is a problem not worth fixing.

CONCLUSION

Outlined in this article are some best practices from the book Innovation Demystified Tapping into our creative core. A more comprehensive set of tools and techniques are covered in the full book text which is available on **Amazon.co.uk**

I encourage you to sit down and speak with your staff about these vital issues the future of your company depends on it.

REFERENCE

Innovation demystifed Tapping into our creativie core, by Richard Lawler

About the Author: *Richard is a cross-disciplinary change agent focused on intrapreneurship coaching clients in the areas of Innovation, Creativity and New Business Launches. Both inquisitive and open-minded, seeing around the corner and thinking laterally are Richard's value adds. Collaboratively and diplomatically, he designs sustainable Win-Win scenarios. Mentally, he is perceptive, nurturing, and supportive.*

*These factors make him suitable for the 21st Century Knowledge Economy as a thought leader. Author of **Innovation Demystified: Tapping into your creative core**.*

Richard holds a Master's Degree in Business/Entrepreneurship and Bachelor's in IT Management from Dundalk Institute of Technology. For a consultation please email - richard@startinnovationg.ie

13. GLIDE: Innovation is a Choice
by *Dr. Susan Harwood*

EXECUTIVE SUMMARY

GLIDE and GLIDE-ing contain several elements with an innovation process applicable to individuals and organizations of all types and sizes.   GLIDE encourages everyone to recognize their own innovation potential, build fun and excitement back into personal and professional life through innovation/creation, and ignite the fire of enthusiasm for ideas through the eyes of childlike wonder. Gliding blooms in the interconnections of the heart and mind of an individual or in the hearts and minds of employees and volunteers.

INTRODUCTION

Why is innovation important?? Innovation is the heartbeat of invention, of creation, and of moving (or gliding!) to something new and exciting. We love innovation for the same reason we love leaders and entrepreneurs: they take us places we want to go, but didn't know we wanted to go there until we arrived!!

Innovation is a Choice – a choice everyone and anyone can make. Innovation does not require permission, approval by the CEO, friends or relatives… but it does require desire, passion, and clarity of purpose. Innovation is totally dependent upon the individual innovator (or group of innovators), either from within an organization or as independent agents. The most successful new inventions (process, product, or service inventions) had innovation and innovators all along the path from idea or concept through marketing   and   sales.

What is Innovation?
An organizational culture can be described as the crown jewel in the heartbeat of each employee, whatever their role (leader, manager, line, or staff) as they begin each new day. It is demonstrated in how and what they say, and how they treat one another. In how resources are spent, how people are viewed as either assets or expense items

not in the times of great success, but in the times of profit struggle and growth. An organization's true culture is revealed during these times of challenge.

This same description of an organizational culture can be applied to an individual, a single person. We often refer to these as values. Underlying every culture, be it organizational or personal, are the values that drive all decision making. Through these values, we measure ourselves and others; through these values, we prioritize how we spend our time and money. Through these values, we decide where we will focus our innovative talent each and every day.

Innovation blooms and thrives in the interconnections between the hearts and minds of employees. At times, innovation is a feeling.....a feeling which can lead to the creation of something new – something that might initially look significant or trivial from the lens of the bottom line of the organization, but of paramount significance to the innovator. There are many times that the passion of the innovator causes them to leave the comfort of the organization start a new organization – a new business, a non-profit, a new enterprise – that will foster their idea. Many of the most successful companies and non-profit organizations in the world started just this way.

Innovation is occurring when you are so excited by a project that everyone involved feels the high energy, feels fully engaged in the excitement of creating something new, something that the team believes in.

At other times, innovation is in the quiet satisfaction of the individual discovering a new sequence to an existing procedure that no one has thought of before, but that can and will make a big difference in efficiency and effectiveness.

Trust, truth, open exchanges of ideas, employees encouraging one another, building on one another's ideas, and reduced complications in the management processes freeing minds to explore the possible are some of the elements prospering where you find on-going sustainable innovation in organizations.

BUT....Innovation does not require permission. All that is required are individuals who are <u>willing to innovate</u>.

When an individual is faced with more month left than money, innovative ways to stretch the food budget, or rearranged the sequence of bill payments. This is innovation at work.

"Necessity is the mother of invention". People are often their most innovative when faced with what limited traditional options have to offer. We see this as being thrifty, but facing a tough reality and finding new ways to deal with it – this is also innovation.

Terminology Versatility or Blockages
"What's in a name?" William Shakespeare once asked this very insightful question. We apply terms or names to concepts, people, places, products, and services. Once we apply the name, we modify its meaning. At one time, the term "cool" referred to the temperature outside, and a mouse was a small rodent, and an apple was a crisp fruit. These terms can evoke feelings. Innovators can align familiar words with clever ways to capture and express a new idea and the feelings the new concept can invoke.

Marketing departments have found wonderful "reuses" for our words. Smart new uses for words, or creative ways to reinvent words into new forms, it depends on your perspective. The original forms are still perfectly intact, but the new application of the words allow for an expansion of their meanings.

There are many examples of terminology overlap as well. Where on the continuum of size does small turn into medium, and medium turn into large? The answer is, it depends – on how we choose to define these terms, on what we want to align with each term in order to associate the term with the feeling. If the customer feels larger is better – rename the medium size popcorn container "small", rename the original "large" popcorn to "medium, and bring in a newer, larger "large" and an even larger "jumbo". If the customer thinks a smaller product is better, name your smallest new iPod product "nano" to invoke a feeling of incredible smallness.

Similarly, the words innovate and create…a great deal of effort that has gone into carefully defining the differences in these two words to enable a clear discussion about which term we mean when. So, with the original definitions of create and innovate still perfectly intact (and you have the freedom to choose what definitions you would like to choose), in our context of GLIDE these actions blend together. Both are still active - but intertwined. Simplification is the reason.

When we are going through the process of innovation, there is an element of creation - and vice versa. The blending of these ideas is a natural way to expand our ideas and outputs. As children, it came so easily to us. Over time, we learned the "right answer" too well – and it tends to tarnish the excitement we felt as children to color the trees purple… and laugh.

Figure 13.1: GLIDE-ing Continuum © potencia, inc. 2012

The *GLIDE-ing* continuum: We innovate when we create and we create when we innovate.

create   innovate

The Balancing Question for Organizations

Companies struggle with the paradox of generating innovation. Figure 13.2 shows the four variables in constant discussion when the act of innovation is not aligned with or perhaps somewhat in conflict with the organization's culture. A culture high in terms of "control" with lots of policies, rules, and theory x management - tends to emphasize strict oversight during the gestation and scenario planning of the ideas.

The organization and its management imply deep concern or even fear that the "innovators" will run wild and free...coming up with products totally not in line with either the current product portfolio or that would require too many resources to bring to market. *(note: the word "product" in this section can refer to products, services or processes)* These concerns could certainly come to pass, but if these become the guiding principles for developing innovative products which lead to the long term sustainability of the firm, then perhaps the wrong issues are being addressed. In fact, many organizations with this type of culture tend to locate their people focused on innovation in a different building, part of town, a different part of the country or a different country. These remote groups establish a culture conducive to the act of creating and innovating.

The inverse can also be problematic Research by Pelz and Andre showed that 100 percent autonomy in engineering organizations can have the same impact to productivity as zero autonomy. The highest rate of success occurs in the range of 75-85% autonomy. Measuring or building a culture's percent autonomy can be challenging, but the key is to understand how much standardization is helpful and leads to innovative talent being focused on the creation of the new ideas, rather than consumed in the arguments of the selection of tools, or reinventing management processes.

Balancing these variables becomes part of the art of development. This is also true for start-ups, which tend to err more in the "too much" category of flexibility and autonomy. As ideas ease through the maturity cycle from inkling to prototype, the balance begins to shift from autonomy and flexibility, to control and structure.

Note: The innovation process for individuals and organizations is covered in detail in the GLIDE book, available January 2013, www.glideonline.co.

The Balancing Question for Individuals

Sound complicated? Most things do seem more complicated when viewed in a larger scale, but as an individual looking at your own innovative ideas, it can be really quite simple. You have full autonomy out of the gate, but as you glide along the pathway to solidify your initial idea, the balancing questions can become tools to keep you focused - yet flexible.

First set of question: What problem are you trying to solve that the traditional or known solution is no longer useful? Once you have this in mind, jot it down (a sentence or two should be plenty).

Second question: What are your possible solutions? Don't edit away possibilities (yes, this is a form of brainstorming for one person). Now comes the most important part......sleep on it. Before you go any further, give you mind a gestation period of one or two nights sleep. This gives the rest of our thinking tools, our subconscious, time to participate. I find my solutions much richer - and develop several more ideas I had not considered - after some sleep.

Third set of questions: What are the benefits of each solution? Which one appeals to me the most? What is my gut saying to me? Your intuition is a great guide. If you have not yet met the voice of your intuition, stop right here. No really, stop. Go sit quietly in a place no one can see you and you can hear no noise. Close your eyes, take a deep breath, and quiet your mind and ask to hear the voice of your intuition. No seriously, sit still, if you really want to feel your intuition and recognize it. Now, as you are walking back to your reading spot, notice which solution "feels" right. Don't analyze it!!! What feels right?

For lots of folks, they are great friends with their intuition. They have learned to trust it even when the facts seem to be saying something else.

This is your internal DNA-GPS and it serves as a wonderful guide. If the first time you met your intuition was a few minutes ago (and you totally thought that exercise was bogus), well - keep an open frame of mind. More successful ideas were started by hunches and gut feelings (synonyms for intuition) than through analysis.

Fourth set of questions: What will it take to implement the solution you and your intuition selected in step 3? Who do you need to gather some additional information from? You may want to take your top two solutions and analyze the cost implications. Cost can be time, money, or space available. Is there a solution you just know (intuitively) it's "the one" - regardless of cost? Then what would it take to implement it? Now we could be back to asking the questions in the first set again to help us glide through implementation.

Once you have the analysis complete, you are ready to implement. Simple balancing the 4 variables as you went gliding along the innovation process.

FIGURE 13.2: GLIDE-The Balancing Question

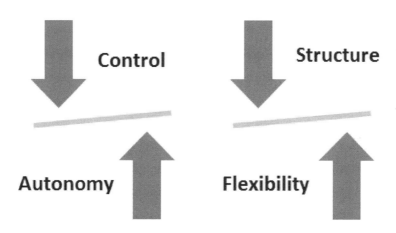

The GLIDE-ing Innovation Question: How much??

Control Structure

Autonomy Flexibility

© potencia, inc 2012

Barriers to Innovation
This section could easily have been titled "the case of too much pressure". There is a rhythm to **gliding**. Space, gestation time, the art of resourcing the idea or new product; just enough to keep it going; not enough to sink it (yes, too much money, too soon can stop the progress of innovation before it ever gets to prototype stage) are carefully balanced aspects to gliding. There is strength in the struggle that can only be attained through the struggle. You can't train it, or buy, or replicate it…..only experience it.

Lessons in Gliding from a Farmer
When we want to understand the best practices of a process, most of us look for someone who has been continually successful at that particular process and we seek information.

I did not say guidance or help because typically we want to know how they did it so we can replicate it in our own way. To illustrate this point, I choose the profession that spends more time growing products than any other profession - the farmer.

Here are tips that farmers would share on ways to impede the progress of growth:

- Digging up a seed to look at its progress
- Standing over a new seedling preventing the sun from getting through
- Yelling at the seedling to grow faster
- Ignoring the seedling causing it to die of lack of water or nutrition
- Cutting the seedling before it is fully ready for harvest
- Not replanting thinking there is plenty of bounty
- Not remembering that it all started with a seed.

Exercise: That was my idea first!
What is a great idea you had first, that turned out great---for someone else? Why was it a great idea? What prevented you from pursuing it? Take a few minutes to think about that really super idea you had. Remember how great it felt when it came to you. Your heart beat a little faster. You couldn't help smiling to yourself. Did you start to plan how you could make it happen or who you needed to get some information from to make it an even better idea?

You just knew it was a great idea, but.....then you talked yourself out of it, or you let someone else talk you out of it. Friends and family usually mean well, but have stopped many people from pursing their greatness ideas because IT'S NOT THEIR IDEA!!

What did you learn from that experience? What is the worst that could happen to you if you pursue your own great ideas? Will you die? Will you be hated? Will you be bankrupt? Will you be hurt? Will you hurt someone else? Will you be embarrassed? Will you be laughed at? Will your friends desert you? Are you just too lazy? Do you not know what to do next? **OR** will you be successful? Often the fear of success is the greatest barrier of all.

These may seem like tough questions, and they are, but they are the questions to ask if you continually have ideas but do not take action to make your idea a reality.

CONCLUSION

How many amazing innovative ideas never make it to market because innovation is not "*GLIDE-ing*" along each element of the process? Innovative engineers but ho hum marketing.....Great marketing, but ho hum ideas (although great marketing can certainly sell non innovation....and non-innovative products do make money, but this is typically not a sustainable profit model).

"In every job that must be done, there is an element of fun..." - Mary Poppins, extraordinary governess dreamed up by writer P.L.Travers
......and the potential to glide!!

REFERENCES

Pelz, D., and Andrews, F., (1999). **Scientists in Organizations: Productive Climates for Research and Development.** John Wiley and Sons, Inc.

*About the Author: Susan is an energizing professional who transform business, leadership, and organizations. Through her firm, **Potencia, Inc.** founded in 2000 (www.potenciaconsulting.com), she develops innovative solutions through her unique blend of strong academic credentials; successful global business experience; international entrepreneurial research projects, and clarity of purpose. Hundreds of Fortune 500 and National Laboratory leaders have been developed through her leadership academies and personal coaching.*

Katzenback's book, __The Wisdom of Teams__, the London Times, and the Human Resources Executive have written of her system's approach to organizational design and learning. Clients include, new venture start-ups, Lockheed, DOE, Telespazio, Los Alamos National Laboratory, Medtronic, IMTI, and Motorola. She is described as "intellectually-agile, visionary, passionate, articulate, astute, and action oriented". As a captivating speaker and facilitator, Susan inspires and challenges individuals to unleash the power of their potential.

As Project Manager for the Irish Executive Press, she led the integration of 14 leading practitioners' contributions to create __Best Practices for Success Business__ available at __www.irishexecutive.com__. Currently, she is completing 3 publication projects: __New Life Lifestyles: Rethinking how we live__ www.newlifestyles.me) release date fall 2012; __GLIDE: Unleashing the Innovation within__ with co-author Dr. Eric Maass, (www.glideonline.co); and __GLIMMER: Creating Competitive Advantage through Learning__ , (www.glimmeronline.com), release dates Spring 2013.

Susan's credentials include: PhD and MA, Fielding Graduate University specializing in the Psychology of Leadership; a MGA specializing in Organizational Processes, University of Maryland, European Division; and a BS in Technical Education, University of Akron.

14. Lean: What Executives Should Know
by *Dr. Eric Maas*

EXECUTIVE SUMMARY

Lean can provide substantial benefits – but executives can be confused by the jargon and the benefits and potential issues. Executives can lead appropriately once they understand what benefits to expect, what experts to respect, and what cautions and red flags to intercept and deflect. A simple test can help determine whether Lean, Six Sigma, or Design for Six Sigma will be the most beneficial in addressing the organization's constraint. Lean is the most beneficial if manufacturing cycle time, inventory, or other wastes are holding the organization back. A few cautions are introduced, along with some lean terminology – must of it derived from Japanese terms used in Toyota. Some key Lean tools and best practices either associated with or venturing to advanced industrial engineering methods that extend beyond Lean methods are briefly introduced.

INTRODUCTION

Lean, Six Sigma, Lean Six Sigma, Lean Sigma, Design for Six Sigma, Design for Lean Sigma, DMAIC, DMADV, DMADOV…when a leader wants to drive his or her organization to the next level and beyond, the terminology is often confusing. Some experts almost seem to be exploiting the confusion to sell you the approach that, coincidentally, is what they specialize in.

Let's look behind the foggy curtain and clearly – and simply - define the terminology, provide a simple test to decide what is most appropriate for your organization as it stands today – and use that understanding to plot a course that will succeed in meeting the expectations you've set.

A SIMPLE TEST

Looking at the business that includes your manufacturing line, what is holding you back? What is holding back your financial results now, and restraining you from achieving your vision for the future? With these simple questions, you and your leadership team are applying Eliyahu Goldratt's Theory of Constraints from an enterprise perspective.

Once the executive team has identified the constraint – perhaps with a good deal of analysis from the financial accountants – that constraint can lead to selecting an appropriate approach to overcome the constraint:

- If the constraint is in manufacturing or the broader supply chain, then the Lean methods can provide substantial benefits. Symptoms of this type of constraint include having more demand than you can satisfy, reducing your market share primarily because you are too slow to fulfil orders and/or have insufficient capacity to handle the demand. The factory is running near capacity, but things are getting clogged up, cycle times are high and rising, and you are searching for space – for space to store ever-increasing work-in-process inventory.

- If the constraint is in yield or defects (or quality or reliability) on existing products, then the Six Sigma / DMAIC (Define – Measure – Analyze – Improve – Control) methods can help teams focus on finding and clearly defining the issues, and then improving the situation by reducing variability or reducing defects, and sustain the improvements. The issue will often show up in Cost of Quality metrics, but also in rework loops and low yields.

- If the constraint is in marketing or product development, then the DFSS approach may prove valuable. In this situation, your manufacturing is running at lower utilizations or per cent of capacity than you would hope, because customers are not rushing to buy your products and perhaps see your products as "me too" compared to your competitors' products.

Note: See Article #14 which clarifies what is meant by Six Sigma (DMAIC) and Design for Six Sigma (DFSS).

LEAN

The term "Lean" almost sells itself. After all, who doesn't want their business to be Lean.. Lean and Mean! ...a Lean Mean Profit Machine?

Lean originated as the Toyota Production System. It was a set of methods and a thought process that was very successful at Toyota, and often provides similar benefits to manufacturing (and non-manufacturing areas). The term "Lean" was coined and rapidly adopted in the USA.

While the term "Lean" might imply that cost reduction is the primary focus for these methods – Lean is actually focused on reducing waste, and thereby improving manufacturing cycle time or lead time.

Lean identifies several types of wastes (see Table 14.a), but a key focus is on inventory reduction – because a reduction in Work-In-Process (WIP) inventory leads directly to a reduction in Cycle Time...as described by Little's Law:

Cycle Time = WIP / Throughput

Table 14.a: Seven Types of Waste ("Muda" in Japanese)

Inventory (all components, work in process and finished product not being processed
Transport (moving products that are not actually required to perform the processing)
Motion (people or equipment moving or walking more than is required to perform the processing)
Waiting (waiting for the next production step)
Overproduction (production ahead of demand)
Over Processing (resulting from poor tool or product design creating activity)

Defects (the effort involved in inspecting for and fixing defects)

Caution 1:   In many standard Cost Accounting systems, Inventory appears on the Asset side of the ledger.   Just when the team implementing Lean on their first pilot effort and are happily celebrating their brilliant first success in reducing WIP inventory - and you are celebrating their success… the accountants may be point out that the reduction in inventory has been reflected in unfavourable financial results - due to a sudden drop in assets.

Caution 2: Several Lean methods are focused on "low hanging fruit". They provide short term, often dramatic gains…but, eventually, the team may have picked the fruit and begin wondering "what   comes   next".

Shortly before this point of diminishing returns seem often to be the precise moment where the expensive consultant will present the bill, smile a dazzling smile,   and hurry off to the next manufacturing company replete with a virtual cornucopia of fruit strewed over the field of clovers.

Caution 3: Lean experts tend to adopt Japanese terminology, which seems to convey a sense of mystical knowledge. Terms like "Muda", "Kanban", "Gemba", "Hoshin Kanri", "Poka Yoke", and "Kaizen Events" begin to weave their way into the otherwise cheery brogue of normal conversations.

Lean Terminology from Japan: Here is a quick translator for each of these terms:

Muda – Waste (see the table of 7 types of waste above)

- **Kanban** – One method of implementing a "Pull System", whereby material requisitioned from a prior step using a system of cards reflecting the need to pull material from the prior   operation.

   Noteworthy insight: The book, Factory Physics (Hopp & Spearman, 2011), documents studies that have shown that the benefits of a "Pull System" can be achieved without the complex system of cards, but by simply setting an appropriate maximum level for the WIP. The authors refer to this simpler approach as "CONWIP" for "Constant WIP" or Constant Work-in Process.

- **Gemba (or Genba)** – this word translates to "the real place"; this commonly refers to visiting the manufacturing floor to see what's really happening and to gather information.
- **Hoshin Kanri** – a Japanese term that corresponds to strategic planning or strategic deployment.
- **Poka Yoke** – the original term apparently was "Baka Yoke", which translates to "Idiot-proofing". There is a story where Shigeo Shingo, the inventor of many methods in the Toyota Production System, used the term "Baka Yoke" when he was in a manufacturing area, and one of the workers became upset, taking it as if the great Shigeo Shingo had called her an idiot. The term was rapidly replaced with the more diplomatic term, "Poka Yoke", which means mistake proofing – or, more precisely, preventing inadvertent mistakes. The goal of Poka Yoke is to develop simple, inexpensive methods for a step in the manufacturing process such that it is either impossible or very difficult to make a mistake in the first place...and/or if a mistake starts to occur, it will be detected immediately and rectified.
- **Kaizen Events** – the term "Kaizen" translates as "change for the good". A Kaizen Event or Kaizen Blitz is not an unfortunate juxtaposition of terms from former axis powers in World War II, but rather a description of a structured meeting of people involved in a manufacturing process with a focus on process improvement. Often times, many of the most effective cost reductions come out of a Kaizen Event.

BEST PRACTICES

While many of the tools in the Lean toolkit are derived from the Toyota Manufacturing System, some have roots from the assembly line concepts developed at Ford Motor Company in the early 20th Century and others from general Industrial Engineering best practices.

The latter includes the concept of Standard Work, while the former includes concepts now adopted as "TAKT time" to synchronize manufacturing steps to the demand rate.

Tools related to factory layout include:

- **Spaghetti Diagram**, in which the team measures the actual distance material, travels from start to finish ....often a surprisingly long distance. The team then considers alternate layouts for the factory floor which reduce the total distance travelled by the material.

-

- **Value Stream Mapping (VSM),** a rather useful process map that shows important information like where Inventory is held, and translates the quantity of material to the time the material must waits in inventory before being processes. The sums of value-added time and non-value added time, and total manufacturing time are summarized, and the opportunities to shorten total manufacturing time are often clearly exposed through this step. Some Lean experts claim that Value Stream Mapping was a relatively minor tool for the Toyota Production Systems, but it has been found remarkably useful for many manufacturing and non-manufacturing processes.

- **5S** – which stands for 5 Japanese terms that have an S-like initial sound. These 5 Japanese terms translate into a sequence of steps that help make the factory floor more....clean. Yes, 5S is basically a step-by-step formula for cleaning up the factory floor, and putting everything into its appropriate place, and removing things that don't belong on the factory floor. as discrete event simulation (using Simul8, for example) allow the team to explore alternative methods on a simulator before embarking on the rather expensive and often somewhat problematic steps of trying ideas out on the factory floor.

Some of these more advanced methods will be explored in future articles. Some companies have extended the Lean concepts to more advanced methods from Industrial Engineering – such as concepts from the book, Factory Physics, which include equations and graphs that allow a company to quickly assess how well the factory is performing on key metrics compared to the Best Possible Case, Worst Case, and Practical Worst Case. Sophisticated methods such

CONCLUSION

Armed with some insight into the methods, terminology, benefits and pitfalls of Lean manufacturing approaches, executives can cut through the jargon and confusion to explore the value of Lean to their business.

REFERENCES

James Womack, Daniel Jones, Daniel Roos, *The Machine That Changed the World : The Story of Lean Production*, Harper Perrenial, 1991.
Wallace Hopp and Mark Spearman , *Factory Physics*, Waveland Press, 2011.
Eric Maass and Patricia McNair, *Applying Design for Six Sigma to Software and Hardware Systems,* Prentice-Hall, 2009.
Eliyahu Goldratt, *Haystack Syndrome*, North River Press, 1990.

About the Author: Dr. Maass was a co-founder of the Six Sigma methods at Motorola and the key *advocate for the focus on Variance Reduction. He developed Yield Surface Modeling, a patented method for multiple response optimizations that resulted in over 60 first pass successful new products, and was the Lead Master Black Belt for DFSS at Motorola. His most recent book, Applying DFSS to Software and Hardware Systems, provides clear step-by-step guidance on applying DFSS for developing innovative and compelling new products and technologies, while managing the business, schedule and technical risks.*

Eric's roles at Motorola included Research and Development through Manufacturing, to Director of Operations for a $160 Million business and Director of Design and Systems Engineering. Most recently, Eric developed Medtronic's DFSS / DRM Black Belt curriculum and program receiving the Medtronic Star of Excellence, the highest recognition in the company

Eric received his Bachelor's degree in Biological Sciences from the University of Maryland Baltimore County, his Master's degree in Biomedical Engineering from Arizona State University and his PhD degree in Industrial and Systems Engineering from Arizona State University.

15. Design for Six Sigma: What Every Executive Should Know by Dr. Eric Maass

EXECUTIVE SUMMARY

A previous article provided an overview and a simple test to determine whether Lean, Six Sigma, or Design for Six Sigma will be most beneficial in addressing the organization's constraint. Design for Six Sigma can help the organization develop compelling new products, new services, new software or new technology that meets or exceeds the customers' expectations. It also can help in developing a new process, a new tool or a new method

INTRODUCTION

Design for Six Sigma provides an approach to develop new products, processes, technologies, software or services, through these aspects:

- Identify and manage a set of key requirements necessary and sufficient to satisfy customer's and stakeholder's expectations, that are unambiguous, verifiable and clearly understood by the development team.
- Flow down the prioritized requirements; engage suppliers as partners.
- Use predictive engineering and optimization, coupled with risk management, to ensure the product and its components are robust to manufacturing variation and use conditions, and are predicted to meet or exceed expectations and to achieve high yield and high reliability over the range of use conditions, throughout the life cycle.
- Verify that the new product is capable of fulfilling requirements under normal and stressful use conditions, and manufacturable with high, consistent yield and high reliability.

DFSS is applicable to development projects involving a variety of engineering disciplines. Mechanical engineers can apply DFSS in developing simple mechanical devices (like scissors) or a complex mechanical system (like a motorcycle) or an electromechanical system (such as a motor or generator). A team of biomedical engineers, electrical engineers, and mechanical engineers can use DFSS to handle the complex requirements for a prosthetic hand.

In several cases, DFSS has been applied to services; published recommendations for applying DFSS to services focus on a subset of the more comprehensive DFSS approach that start with gathering the Voice of the Customer (VOC) and developing measurable requirements, but then focus on developing confidence that the customers will be satisfied with the quality and responsiveness of the service . This approach can apply to some software projects, such as IT projects that focus on providing services.

In situations where new product development involves software and hardware development (Figure 1), requirements may be flowed down and addressed by separate software and hardware development teams. By its nature, software depends on hardware, and the performance of the hardware tends to depend on the software. The hardware and software interactions and interfaces pose challenges that can be addressed by integrating software and hardware teams, by using effective emulation, or by empowering teams to focus on the hardware and software interfaces and interactions.

Figure 15.1: A cellular phone as an example of a system involving both hardware and software

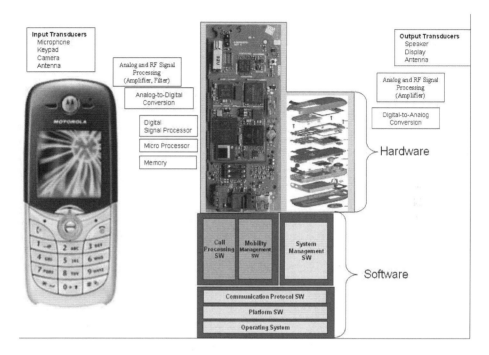

For a complex electronic system, high-level requirements are flowed down and allocated to hardware and software aspects that can be addressed by those with the appropriate expertise, while supporting the ability of the team to address the interactions and interfaces involved. Teams may focus on a subset of the requirements – the most challenging requirements that involve measurable parameters are referred to as Critical Parameters. The allocation of the critical parameters to subsystems, functions, and components is referred to as Critical Parameter flow-down. Critical Parameter flow-up involves prediction of the capabilities for the Critical Parameters; the process from flow down through flow up of optimized critical parameters is referred to as Critical Parameter Management. The DFSS flow for a complex electronic system is illustrated by Figure 2. Figure 3 shows the DFSS flow for a software development project involving existing hardware.

Figure 15.2: DFSS Flow for an electronic system involving both software and hardware

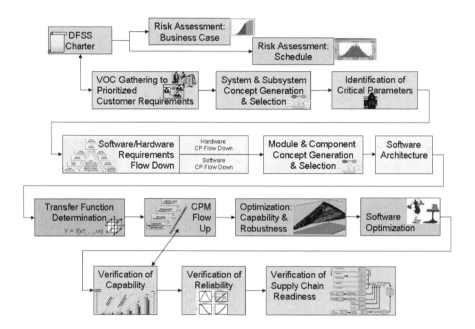

Figure 15.3: DFSS Flow for a software development project using existing hardware

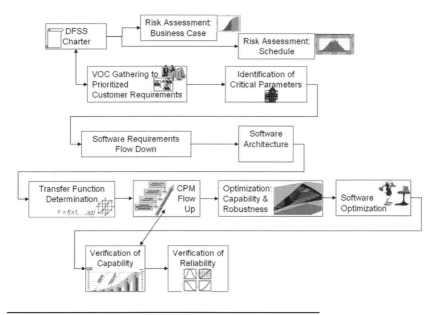

DFSS Process Nomenclatures

DMAIC has become recognized as the standard sequence of steps for process or business improvement and problem-solving aspects of Six Sigma.

By contrast, no standard process has emerged for Design for Six Sigma (DFSS). Alternative DFSS process nomenclatures include Identify Design Optimize Verify (IDOV), Concept Design Optimize Verify (CDOV), and Concept Design Optimize Control (CDOC™), which involve the Identify or Concept phase, the Design phase, the Optimize Phase and the Verify or Control phase. Define Measure Analyze Design Verify (DMADV) and Define Measure Analyze Design Optimize Verify (DMADOV) nomenclatures share the Define, Measure and Analyze phases of DMAIC.

Software practitioners in the industry suggested a nomenclature for DFSS that used terms commonly used during development. These engineers suggested the terms Requirements, Architecture, Design,

Integrate, Optimize, and Verify. This nomenclature provides an easily remembered mnemonic, RADIO-V. The alignment of RADIOV with the DFSS Flow is shown in figure 4. Key tools, methods, and deliverables are shown in Table 1. (DFSS Flowchart: **http://6sigmaexperts.com** .)

Figure 15.4: Alignment of RADIOV with the DFSS Flow

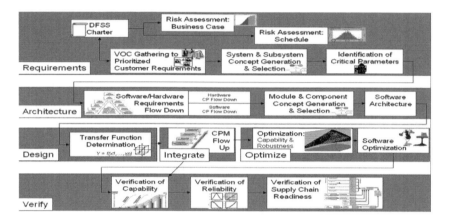

Table 15.a: Key DFSS tools and methods associated with steps for CDOV, DMAD(O)V and RADIOV.

DFSS Step	DFSS Processes			Key Tools and Methods
	CDOV	DMADV	RADIOV	
DFSS Charter				DFSS Charter, Deployment Plan
Business Case: Risk Management				Monte Carlo Simulation - Business Case
Schedule: Risk Management				Monte Carlo Simulation - Critical Chain / TOC-PM
VOC Gathering	Concept	Define	Requirements	Concept Engineering, KJ Analysis, Kano Analysis, Interviews, Surveys, Conjoint Analysis, Customer Requirements Ranking
System Concept Generation & Selection				Brainstorming, TRIZ, System Architecting, Axiomatic Design, Unified Modeling Language (UML), Pugh Concept Selection
Identification of Critical Parameters		Measure		Quality Function Deployment (QFD), Design Failure Modes and Effects Analysis (DFMEA), Fault Tree Analysis (FTA)
Critical Parameter Flow Down	Design	Analyze	Architecture	Quality Function Deployment (QFD), Critical Parameter Management, Fault Tree Analysis (FTA), Reliability Model
Module or Component Concept Generation and Selection				Brainstorming, TRIZ, System Architecting, Axiomatic Design, Universal Modeling Language (UML), Pugh Concept Selection
Software Architecture				Quality Attribute Analysis, Universal Modeling Language (UML), Design Heuristics, Architecture Risk Analysis, FMEA, FTA, Simulation, Emulation, Prototyping, Architecture Tradeoff Analysis Method (ATAM)
Transfer Function Determination			Design	Existing or Derived Equation, Logistic Regression, Simulation, Emulation, Regression Analysis, Design of Experiments (DOE), Response Surface Methodology (RSM)
Critical Parameter Flow Up and Software Integration	Optimize	Design	Integrate	Monte Carlo Simulation, Generation of System Moments Method, Software Regression, Stability and Sanity Tests
Capability and Robustness Optimization			Optimize	Multiple Response Optimization,Robust Design, Variance Reduction, RSM, Monte Carlo Simulation with Optimization
Software Optimization				DFMEA, FTA, Software Mistake Proofing, Performance Profiling, UML, Use Case Model, Rayleigh Model, Defect Discovery Rate
Software Verification			Verify	Software testing
Verification of Capability	Verify	Verify		Measurement System Analysis (MSA), Process Capability Analysis, McCabe Complexity Metrics
Verification of Reliability				Reliability Modeling, Accelerated Life Testing (ALT), WeiBayes, Fault Injection Testing
Verification of Supply Chain Readiness				Design for Manufacturability and Assembly (DFMA), Lead Time and On Time Delivery Modeling, Product Launch plan, FMEA/FTA for Product Launch

DFSS has a wide range of applicability and can be relevant for a variety of engineering disciplines and interdisciplinary efforts. The RADIOV process, which was proposed by software practitioners, provides a comprehensive process that is flexible enough for simple or complex projects for developing software, systems, technologies, and services. A DFSS flowchart provides guidance for practitioners as they develop a robust, reliable product. Relevant case studies can be found in the book referenced below.

REFERENCE

Eric Maass and Patricia McNair, *Applying Design for Six Sigma to Software and Hardware Systems,* Prentice-Hall, 2009.Eliyahu Goldratt, *Haystack Syndrome*, North River Press, 1990.

About the Author: Dr. Maass was a co-founder of the Six Sigma methods at Motorola and the key *advocate for the focus on Variance Reduction. He developed Yield Surface Modeling, a patented method for multiple response optimizations that resulted in over 60 first pass successful new products, and was the Lead Master Black Belt for DFSS at Motorola. His most recent book, Applying DFSS to Software and Hardware Systems, provides clear step-by-step guidance on applying DFSS for developing innovative and compelling new products and technologies, while managing the business, schedule and technical risks.*

Eric's roles at Motorola included Research and Development through Manufacturing, to Director of Operations for a $160 Million business and Director of Design and Systems Engineering. Most recently, Eric developed Medtronic's DFSS / DRM Black Belt curriculum and program receiving the Medtronic Star of Excellence, the highest recognition in the company

Eric received his Bachelor's degree in Biological Sciences from the University of Maryland Baltimore County, his Master's degree in Biomedical Engineering from Arizona State University and his PhD degree in Industrial and Systems Engineering from Arizona State University.

16. Implementing Cloud Computing Platforms: Running your business on the cloud-is it possible?
By *Tony O'Dowd*

EXECUTIVE SUMMARY

Cloud based business applications have the potential to redefine the way companies use their IT systems and grow their business. While previously mired in a world of technical complexity and surrounded by expensive IT staff and computer equipment, the modern entrepreneur can deploy cloud-based business applications throughout their organization in a matter of minutes, at a much lower cost. Freeing them up to focus on what they are good at; growing and developing their business idea!

Cloud computing brings immense economies of scale to business applications and delivers computing resources on-demand in much the same way utilities deliver gas and electricity. In the past, companies had to invest ever-growing capital expenditures (CAPEX) in their business applications and to accommodate potential peak loads; they installed huge amounts of capacity. Cloud-computing eliminated the need for this CAPEX expenditure and other related on-going support and management costs.

But the shift to the on-demand model of cloud computing isn't just about cost savings. Far more important, it's about giving organizations the agility they need to act quickly on new opportunities without IT being on the critical path.

INTRODUCTION

You have big ideas. You want to streamline your business and drive sales through the roof like any entrepreneur! But to get there, your ideas need business apps, and business apps have always been too expensive, too complex to install, configure and manage, especially in economic times like these.

A world of complexity

Behind each business app is a world of complexity; They need a data center with office space, power, air conditioning, bandwidth, networks, servers and storage, a complicated application stack and a team of experts to install, configure and run them. You need development, staging, production and fail-over environments.

And when there is a problem…good luck! You call technical support and they don't know so they blame someone else! Oh! And when a new version comes out…..you would upgrade…but that might bring the whole system down! Now this is for one business app, but when you multiply these headaches across a dozen or so apps, it's easy to see why the biggest companies with the best IT departments aren't getting the apps they need.

As an entrepreneur you'd like to install the latest Customer Relations Management (CRM) system or get your sales team to track their leads and opportunities in a Sales Management System, so you can better manage your sales-cycle, however, you've no one on staff with the expertise to install these systems, yet alone the servers and database system required to run them. In this world of complexity, small business doesn't stand a chance!

Cloud Computing – The Solution?

Cloud Computing can provide a better way to run your business. Instead of running your business apps yourself, they run from a shared data center. These data centers contain all the servers and IT expertise to manage these business apps. You just plug in….like a utility. This makes it fast to get started and it costs less.

It's like Gmail, compared to Microsoft Exchange.

> With Gmail do you need servers and storage? **NO!**
>
> Do you need a technical team to keep it up and running? **NO!**
>
> Do you need to do upgrades? **NO!**

When you use any business app that runs in the cloud, you just simply login, customize it and start using it. No special hardware or software is required to access even the most sophisticated business applications. That's the power of cloud-computing!

Think differently – a new business model
This model is so much better; it's changing the way we think about software. Not just for consumer applications but it's also been used for business applications. We call this Enterprise Cloud Computing[7]. Businesses are running all kinds of apps in the cloud these days – accounting, HR, CRM, email, banking – including custom built apps.

Why? Because you can be up and running within a few days, something that was unheard of using traditional business software.
They cost less too, because you don't have to be pay for all the people, products and facilities to run them. The majority of cloud-based business apps are offered using monthly-subscription charges, so subscribers no longer make large CAPEX expenditures when deploying their business apps. And it turns out that they are more scalable, more secure and more reliable than the vast majority of traditional business apps.

Cloud Architecture
Cloud apps are based on an architecture called **multi-tenancy**[8]. With a multi-tenant app, there isn't a copy of the application for each business, its one app that everyone shares. But it's flexible enough to be customized for everyone's business needs.

It's like a giant office building where everyone shares the infra-structure and services like security, lifts, and reception, yet each business can customize their own office space. Business apps are designed to be elastic and can scale to supporting tens of thousands of users or down to only a few.

With a multi-tenant architecture as the back-bone of cloud-based business apps, upgrades and security and performance enhancements can be automatically added at the data-center and you get the benefits immediately. You are always running the latest version of the software with the latest feature set and you don't have to worry about complex upgrades or data management issues.

Paying for the Cloud

Now the way to pay for cloud apps is also different. Forget about buying servers and software, when your apps run in the cloud, you don't buy anything! It's all rolled up into a Predictable Monthly Subscription, so you only pay for what you use. It's just like a utility gas or electric bill…you only pay for what you use!

Finally, cloud-based business apps don't eat up your valuable IT resources so your CFO will love it and you can focus on projects that really impact the business like selling to more clients.

Your business on the cloud

So now we understand cloud computing…the question is "Can you run your business on it!" It's not as big a jump as you would think!

Productivity Applications

Every business needs a word processor, a spread sheet and a presentation app – these are all available on the cloud and are completely free! For instance Google Docs has a word processor, spread sheet and presentations combined into a single business app. And because all of your files are stored in the cloud, you can access you information so matter where you are!

Business email

Email is one of the primary contact services for leads, prospects and clients. For many Microsoft Exchange has been the de-facto standard, however, Google Gmail is a high performance cloud app that is totally customizable for a small business and is provided fee too!

CRM

Sales management is a key productivity and management tool for rapidly growing companies and Salesforce.com is the market leading business app for managing client relationships and sales pipelines. ZOHO CRM is an alternative to Salesforce.com and both are based on the cloud and provide a rich set of features for managing your sales process.

Accounting
The proverbial pain for young entrepreneurs. But yet again, you can now do this on the cloud.(checkout **FreeAgent** or **SortMyBooks)**. Cloud-based accounting apps are highly customizable and freely available for every size of business.

Company Blog
Today's progressive companies are embracing social media and leveraging its power to reach more clients quicker than ever before. A company blog is just one aspect of the social media phenomenon. Try Wordpress.com – you can't get better! For the less technical business owner, setup a www.facebook.com company page. Use this to publish Press Releases, milestone achievements and other corporate news and events.

Social Media
Managing multiple social media sites like Facebook, LinkedIn, Twitter, Google+ can be very time-consuming and challenging for a small business. It can also be complex since all these social media platforms have different interfaces and methods of sharing and disseminating information. Checkout HootSuite for a simple, yet powerful way to manage all these channels in one single interface. It also provides a data analytics capability to track the effectiveness of your social media strategy.

File Sharing
What to share sales brochures, price lists or proposals with your clients, try **Dropbox!** It's another cloud-app that makes sharing files, reports and data with your clients simple and easy. Other cloud-base storage providers are Microsoft SkyDrive and Google Drive and of course the Apple iCloud.

Marcom & Business Materials
Every business needs marketing materials such as business cards,

brochures, logos, flyers complementary slips. Jump into Teak.com, an Irish based cloud-app that puts you in the driving seat and creates all these for you quickly and easily.

Company Backups

If you have valuable files you can't replace, the only real way to protect them is to back them up on a regular basis. Sounds easy, but, it is one of the most basic and overlooked activity of small businesses. Carbonite.com is a cloud-based backup service that makes this task automatic and secure.

Creating an online store for your business

Build a new channel to market for your products by building an online store. Shopify.com is perhaps the best known platform that enables businesses to build online stores in a matter of minutes. Angry Birds uses it!

Online Merchant Accounts

If you've an online store, you'll need an online merchant account. The market leader is PayPal and it makes getting payments from your clients quick and easy.

So the core functions of your business can now be run using the best business apps, all based on the cloud. You don't need any special hardware or software, you don't have to have expensive IT staff to manage your business apps and you can focus on what you do best; driving sales through the roof!

CONCLUSION

Cloud computing brings immense economies of scale to business applications and delivers computing resources on-demand in much the same way utilities deliver gas and electricity. This makes them cheap and easy to deploy in your organization.
But the shift to the on-demand model of cloud computing isn't just about cost savings. Far more important, it's about giving you the agility needed to act quickly on new opportunities without IT being on the critical path.

END NOTES

[1]**Enterprise Cloud Computing**: Refers to running large enterprise scaled applications in data centers and accessing them through the cloud.

[2] **Multi-tenancy**: refers to a principle in software architecture where a single instance of a business app runs on a server, serving multiple client organizations (tenants). This is the opposite to multi-instance architecture, where multiple copies of the business app are running, each instance serving a client organization.

About the Author: Tony is a seasoned serial entrepreneur and intrapreneur having launched successful independent enterprises and large products for major corporations. His most recent ventures include:

In 2000 he formed Alchemy Software Development (www.alchemysoftware.ie), the creators of Alchemy CATALYST and Alchemy PUBLISHER. This company quickly established itself as one of the leading innovators and premium supplier of technology with over 27,000 licenses in use worldwide. Translations.com purchased Alchemy in March 2007.

His new company, Xcelerator, is developing a cloud-based statistical machine translation solution for professional translators. Founded in August 2011, it has already launched its beta-version of KantanMT, a fully scalable, high-speed MT system based on Amazon Web Services and Cloud infra-structure.

In his various career positions as Executive Vice President, Technology Manager, and Software Development Engineer, Tony's expertise lead to the creation of new products and technology for Corel Corporation, Symantec Corporation Lotus Development Corporation.

Tony has a BSC Computer Science from Trinity College Dublin and is a founder of FIT Ltd., a $20 million government training organization for the long term unemployed.

17. Communication: Say it Like You Mean It by *Adrian Rush*

EXECUTIVE SUMMARY

This Best Practice for Communications is to outline the main reason and methods of communication. Also to stress the importance of good and clear communications in business to ensure that there is very little chance of ambiguity and misunderstanding. In business any document produced by a company has to be presented professionally, clearly and in a readable format (style).

INTRODUCTION

This Best Practice for Communications is to outline and explain the various types and methods of communications and why we communicate. In business in order to do anything we have to communicate. Who are we communicating to? In essence we are communicating to three groups of people; these are Staff, Suppliers and Clients.

In all cases clear and concise communication is essential and of the highest importance. Why do we communicate well the simplest answer is to get our message across to people. How do we communicate well there are numerous ways to communicate: Talking (face to face or on a telephone), Writing, Visual.

KEYS TO EFFECTIVE COMMUNICATION

Communications is used so that a person can tell someone else what they are doing, have designed or want them to do. Looking at talking first there are a few questions to ask yourself before you talk.

Talking
When talking it is very important to make sure you think before you talk to ensure that you are confident in the fact that you can get your message across.

- What do we want to say
- How do we say it to make sure you are understood
- How much detail can I give the listener(s)
-

We talk to people all the time and in a non - business it is normally very relaxed and easy to get across your message. You still have to make sure that you are clear in what you are saying and that you are not misunderstood.

Business talking is somewhat different and you have to be sure of your facts and ideas to start with. It is essential that you have your fact correct and that you think what you want to say first. Also it is very important to listen to what is being said to you. Speak clearly so you can be understood.

Most business people end up giving a presentation at some point. This type of talking is stressful and it is very important to make sure you know your subject have good notes.

It is not good practice to have everything you plan to say written down. If it is you are very likely to read the text and not engage with your audience.

You should use notes or headings as pointers and then you will engage with the audience. Change the tone and pitch of your voice otherwise you end speaking in a mono tone and the audience will switch off and not hear or listen to you. Use examples and recant incidents if they are relevant and do not name names of people someone in the audience may know who you are talking about.

Writing
There are several types of writing and although essentially they are trying to achieve the same end result they are all different.

- Make sure you write so everyone can understand what you have said
- Present it so it easy to read

- Understand the needs of your reader
- Do not write long complicated paragraphs
- Do not edit or review something you have written

Very broadly there are two types of writing Fiction and Business. The focus of this section is Business. The most important thing to remember with writing is to have good and clear presentation. This is because if a reader cannot follow or see what they want they will stop reading after a couple of minutes.

Business Writing can roughly be broken into smaller groups and these are:

- Letters, E-mails, Invoices, Statements Receipts and Notes
- Reports, Manuals (Handbooks), Business Plans
- Sales Brochures, Catalogues
- Tender Requests and Tender Responses

Letters, E-mails, Invoices, Statements Receipts and Notes: All of these are relatively short and are used to impart information quickly and briefly. Invoices, Statements and Receipts are used when work has been done for a client and payment is being asked for or has been received. Letters and E-mails are used to ask someone to do something or to accompany other more detailed information.

When writing Reports, Manuals (Handbooks) or Tenders having a good format that is easy to follow and to read will keep the reader engaged and interested. One thing that many people are afraid of is to have white space on a page. There is nothing wrong in having white space and if the person writing uses BS 4884 Technical Manuals there will be white space on your pages. With computers you can set up your own Style Sheets and Templates for commonly produced documents; this speeds up the process and ensures a commonality in a business's documents. With computers it is possible to get them to produce contents lists and other things and it is up to the individual if you choose to use them.

Reports, Manuals (Handbooks), Business Plans: Each of these has specific purposes. A Business Plan is used by a business to set out what it plans to do and what its aims are. It is most used by a new business starting up and is normally of greatest interest to people who are being asked to invest in the new venture.

Reports can come in a variety of styles and this will depend on the requirements. One type is an annual financial report for a business which shows how that business has performed for that year. A business may be asked by a client to do some work and produce a report so the client can decide what to do or a report can be requested after an incident has occurred and it may have to go to several different bodies to ensure the incident does not occur again.

Manuals (Handbooks): These come in numerous styles and headings. Most companies if they produce or manufacture an object will have to produce a manual or a suit of manuals. These can be broadly divided into the following headings – Instruction/User Manual; Service/Maintenance Manual and Installation Manual. Each of these will give the reader a different level of information.

The Instruction/User manual has to be written so a non-technical person can use it and set up the piece of equipment easily and quickly.

The Installation Manual is aimed at someone with technical knowledge and a certain level of competence enabling them to install the item and test it having connected it to the appropriate power sources.

The Service/Maintenance Manual is aimed at someone with a high degree of technical knowledge which will enable them to dismantle and repair or replace items within the equipment and re-build it and test it and return it to the customer.

Sales Brochures/Catalogues: These are essentially advertising material for a business. A Sales Brochure gives the reader enough information on the product for them to decide if it is what they want and to go and ask additional questions of a salesman. A catalogue is a complete list of a business's products and it is aimed at showing a potential customer what you can supply and the price.

Tender Request and Tender Responses: These are very specialized documents and require a different approach to other business documents. A Tender Request is prepared by a company or a government department in order to get some work done by a specialist. It should give the specialist enough information to respond to the requirements. A Tender Response is the specialist's response to the Tender Request. A Tender Response should answer all the questions asked of them and be easy to read; well presented; clear and concisely written; factual and highlight the businesses unique selling point

Visual
Visual communications is a complex topic in its own right and yet it is also the easiest to explain. It can be broken down into several sub-groups

Picture – usually artistic and colorful

Drawings – usually line drawings and without any color or limited color

Photographs – a picture of a subject or scene

Pictures will normally have some color in them and can be one two or three dimensional depending on the specific requirements.

Drawings are usually line drawing and will more than likely have no color although they could use shading to highlight specific areas or to hide an area.

Photographs are exactly what they say they are. It is much easier to use photographs with the advent of digital cameras.

There are several formats that a visual can be saved on a computer and it is really up to the person writing the manual to decide what they want and to instruct the person supplying the visual.

With any type of visual being used in a manual it is important make sure that it is relevant to the subject and are put in the correct place in the manual. Every visual must have a title and must be put in the contents list

CONCLUSION

Communication is an essential part of business. All communication from a company is a form of advertising and should be regarded as one of the most important aspects of the business. Whether it is an e-mail or your web site it has to show the company in the best way and yet still be clear and easy to understand and get the message across. It has to be informative and give information to those who want to find out what your company does.

About the Author: *Adrian Rush is a respected seasoned professional the Documentation/Publications Industry. As a qualified Project Manager, Technical Writer, and Editor, his company, AMR Enterprise serves divers multi-national companies in the area of Documentation Consultancy. His clients include British Aerospace, Gilligan Black Recruitment, UTS Parking and Transportation, Hewlett Packard, Pfizer European Financial Shared Services, and Meteor Mobile Communications.*

Most recently, Adrian's focus has been in successful Tender Response and writing a series of Handbooks for running successful businesses. As the Proposal Manager for a LinkedIn Group, his Tender Response Template was the basis for pursing a major project in Shannon.

Adrian attended Wycliffe College Stonehouse Glos England www.amrenterprises.net

Part Three: The People of Your Business

18. Talent Development: An Unexploited Dividend by *Nial O'Reilly*

EXECUTIVE SUMMARY

Any business that requires the involvement of people has a vested interest in understanding and engaging in talent development. Talent development is a process that starts before recruitment and ends only when someone leaves your organization. It incorporates selection, education, training, performance facilitation, leadership and adult development.

It is accepted that people lie at the core of competitive advantage so it follows that every business, small or large, involving people, benefits significantly from having an integrated talent development strategy. To be without one is to miss out on the discretionary effort and potential that each person you employ has to offer and to forego the unparalleled satisfaction that can be derived from helping people realize their full potential. In this short article we will explore the key elements of a best practice talent development strategy.

INTRODUCTION

In his wonderful book 'Good to Great' Jim Collins shares the results of longitudinal research into why some companies break away from their peer group performing at a good level, to become great. Most of the factors shown to contribute to outstanding success in business relate to areas of human influence as opposed to tactical genius.

One of the principles advocated by Jim Collins in 'Good to Great', following his research is **'first who, then what'.** He outlines how important it is to:
- Get the right people on the bus and in the right seats and the wrong people off the bus
- Be rigorous not ruthless
- When in doubt – don't hire
- When you need to make a change – act
- Put your best people on your best opportunities

Having a strategy to select, develop, promote and replace your people is critical to the success of your business and will give you a competitive edge in your market. Leadership of those people in executing the business plan is another key factor.

People come with an enormous level of potential that can be maximized to the mutual benefit of the person and the business they work in. There is an upward spiral of benefits to be derived from organizations facilitating potential in people and people facilitating their own potential to the advantage of the organization. Good Leadership facilitates the maximization of potential in people, teams and businesses.

If you consider that all businesses have three things to spend; **time, money** and **energy** it follows that we should seek to maximize these resources. Most management systems and practices are geared towards maximizing time and money but very few are designed to maximize human energy.

Examine your businesses KPI Report (Key Performance Indicator) and list the number of measures you have for human energy? Most likely you will find that what is being measured in your business is what is easily measurable like the time and money elements. Measuring 'the soft stuff', as it's often called is more difficult so it is often neglected. There seems to be an over emphasis on the tactical elements and insufficient focus on what I call the adaptive elements.

This, I believe, is because we have a leaning, in the Western World at least, towards logical thinking and rely heavily on facts, figures and timing. Visit this short presentation on the Divided Brain to see why this may be the case: http://comment.rsablogs.org.uk/2011/10/24/rsa-animate-divided-brain/

In this short article we will explore some critical elements of a good talent development strategy but first let's look at the present state of talent development in Ireland and the business case for the investment in talent management.

TALENT DEVELOPMENT IN IRELAND

The Forfas Report on Management Development in Ireland published in 2010 and available here: http://www.forfas.ie/media/100316mdc-management-development-in-ireland.pdf defines development for the purposes of the report as 'Any form of training, formal or informal, accredited or non-accredited, which enhances the ability of an SME manager to provide direction, facilitate change, use resources, work with people, achieve results, or manage self or personal skills'. The Council believes that investment in management skills is vital from both a business development perspective and from a human capital perspective.

Figure 18.1: The Spectrum of Talent Development

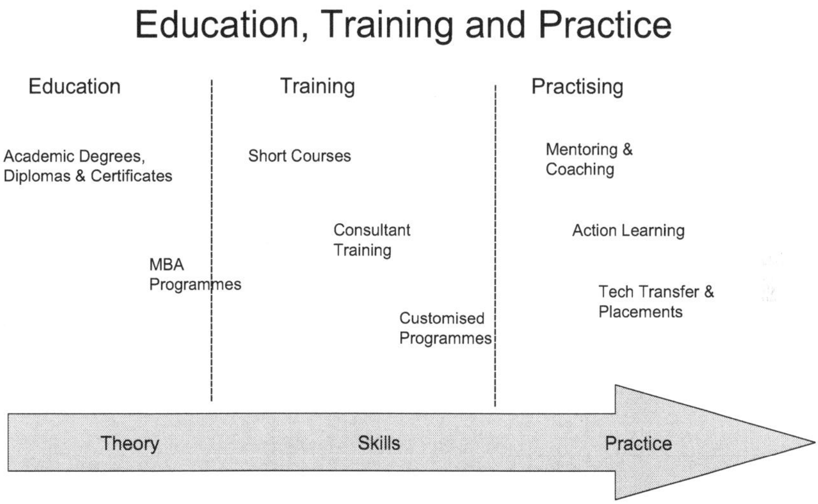

Education, Training and Practice

Education	Training	Practising
Academic Degrees, Diplomas & Certificates	Short Courses	Mentoring & Coaching
	Consultant Training	Action Learning
MBA Programmes		Tech Transfer & Placements
	Customised Programmes	

Theory	Skills	Practice

Adapted from Forfas Report on Management Development in Ireland 2010

This model highlights the range of activities involved in people development.

How are we doing?

The report details Ireland's Current Management Performance and highlights areas for concern. This is an extract from the report:

The Council is particularly concerned with two major issues in relation to management skills:

- *The level of participation in management development amongst SMEs; and*
- *The quality of management development provision.*

The Council is interested in enhancing the quality of management practice amongst SMEs (through improved quality of provision and increased levels of participation) in order to boost firm level productivity and profitability, leading ultimately to enhanced international competitiveness and improved living standards for all. Productivity data reveal that in many sectors, Irish SME productivity performance continues to lag the leading performers. In the manufacturing sector, labor productivity performance amongst Irish SMEs ranks generally in the mid-range of EU-27 ' countries, but is amongst the worst performers of the EU-15 countries.

Reasons to do better
There is ample evidence in the literature and research to prove the value of an effective talent development strategy contributing to improved management practice. A report published jointly by agencies of the Irish and British Government (2009) entitled *'Management Matters in Northern Ireland and Republic of Ireland'* (Available here:
http://www.intertradeireland.com/media/intertradeirelandcom/r
esearchandstatistics/publications/tradeandbusinessdevelopment/
Management%20matters%20in%20Northern%20Ireland%20a
nd%20Republic%20of%20Ireland.pdf)
shows the scale of the opportunity presented by improving talent development is highlighted.

The report states: *'The robust methodology for the evaluation of management practice has enabled its association with corporate performance to be tested and clearly demonstrated. Analysis has shown that management practice scores are closely correlated with a range of corporate performance metrics, including labor productivity, sales growth and return on capital employed.*

The same strong relationships between management practice scores and financial performance hold true across the different countries and cultures surveyed.

Improved management practice is also associated with large increases in productivity and output. ***The findings of the research suggest that a single point improvement in an organization's management practice score is associated with an increase in output equivalent to that produced by a 25% increase in the labor force or a 65% increase in invested capital*** *(Figure 18.2). This observation holds true even after controlling for a variety of factors, including the firm's country, sector and skill level, ownership type, size, profitability to list a few.*

Figure 18.2: Effects of increased factor inputs on output

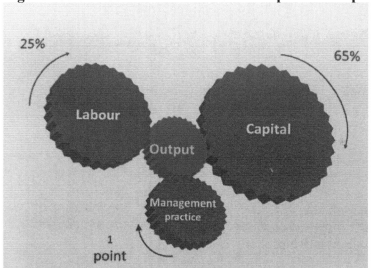

KEY COMPONENTS TO A BEST PRACTICE TALENT DEVELOPMENT STATEGY

Recruitment

As Collins said in 'Good to Great': 'get the right people on the bus'! A robust selection process is paramount. Knowing what you want the job to do is critical before you look for a person to fill it. There are lots of tools and techniques in the market place to help organizations decide what they want in a candidate. Skill, knowledge and ability are the key drivers in selection but behavioral traits should not be ignored.

Role Behavior Analysis is a selection support methodology worth considering. Quick and easy to use on-line, this tool allows a number of people in an organization to profile the role and define what behavioral traits best fit the role. When selection is narrowed down to a short list the candidates can be profiled and a good fit identified. It is rare to find a perfect fit but if you recruit in full knowledge of where the gaps are either in terms of skill, knowledge, ability or behavior this creates a transparent shared platform for performance management when on-boarding is complete.

Performance Facilitation
Optimum performance is facilitated under the following conditions:
- Values
  The values of the organization are clearly understood and are lived particularly by senior   management.
- Vision
  The vision of the organization is clear to everyone and a higher order purpose is at play
- Mission
  The Mission is clear and exciting with detail timelines and milestones regularly reviewed   and up-dated
- Individualized Objectives
  Objectives are agreed with individuals to achieve the mission in the direction of the vision while living up to the values

- Alignment
  Individual objectives are in alignment with the mission, vision and values
- Communication
  Communication is open, regular and three-way (Up, down and around)
- Challenge and Support
  Individual performance is challenged and supported in a dynamic fashion
- Execute
  There is constant focus on execution progress and quality
- Strategic Review
  Progress is strategically reviewed at regular intervals
- Re-plan
  Following strategic reviews the execution plan is revised and up-dated
- The last three steps above are repeated on an on-going basis
- Motivate
  Pay people enough so that money is not an issue then get to know what really motivates   individuals and leverage
- Reward
  Celebrate Success
- Create a '**bility**' culture
  Create a culture where sustaina**bility,** responsi**bility** and accounta**bility** are the norm and   where   reflective learning is an output from failures
- Measure engagement
  If all the above are effective your people will be actively engaged. Measure this regularly   and respond to results

For further information on engagement visit the MacLeod Report 'Engaging for Success'   here:
http://www.bis.gov.uk/files/file52215.pdf

Knowing how your people are, knowing what they want, knowing what they are good at and playing to those strengths are some ways to ensure your people are on a development trajectory.

In his wonderful book Drive, Dan Pink unveils the results of his research into human motivation. Visit a short summary of Pink's findings delivered in a lecture to the RSA here: http://www.youtube.com/watch?v=u6XAPnuFjJc

Leadership

It was once the case that commanding leadership was sufficient to achieve success and it seems that this is no longer the case. Recent developments in the area of emotional intelligence show the shortcomings of an exclusively 'dissonant' style of leadership where command, control and pace setting are the only tools of the one in command. It is now known that great leaders work through emotions. In his book 'The New Leaders' (2002) Daniel Goleman makes the following points: *'Great Leaders move us. They ignite our passion and inspire the best in us. When we try to explain why they are so effective, we speak of strategy, vision, or powerful ideas. But the reality is much more primal: Great leadership works through the emotions.* The good news here is that emotional intelligence can be learned and developed and we have the potential to get more proficient as we get older!

Another reference worth exploring is Heifetz et al *'The Practice of Adaptive Leadership'* (2009) where the fascinating concept of 'the productive zone of dis-equilibrium' is explored. Advocating the need for a mix of dissonant and resonant styles of leadership to promote engagement, productivity and development this is an excellent read for developing leaders.

There are a broad range of skills and competencies required for Leaders to facilitate development some of these include:

- Be a role model
- Display strong personal motivation
- Focus on execution and results
- Understand politics and culture
- Humility
- Resilience
- Success of the business is the focus

Education

Formal education gives people grounding in the fundamentals. Nowadays third level qualifications are the norm with substantial numbers of people staying in education to complete post grad, masters, doctorate and post doctorate qualification. A question arose recently on a blog as to whether it is more advisable to employ an MBA or a PhD. One answer suggested that MBAs no less and less about more and more while PhDs no more and more about less and less! Whatever your perspective on this question there is no doubt that a solid education in a reputable college reduces the risk when hiring. Encouraging your people to continue education throughout their careers is also worth considering.

Ideas on formal education are evolving quickly as demonstrated by this talk by Sir Ken Robinson at TED (2010) entitled 'Bring on the Learning Revolution' http://www.ted.com/talks/sir_ken_robinson_bring_on_the_revolution.html .

Training

Targeted training on the job in skills required for the job is a must to develop your talent and maximize your return on investment in people. It's important to be pragmatic however and ensure that the training will deliver value in the short term. It is also important to ensure that external trainers deliver to your requirements and not just something they have commoditized and prepared in advance.

Practice

What is the difference between training and developmental practice? I like to think of education, training and skills development as the acquisition of tactical knowledge. Metaphorically education, training and skills acquisition is like 'filling a vessel' with knowledge whereas developmental practice helps to 'make the vessel bigger'. This growth of the vessel enables a capacity for increased mental complexity and the acquisition of more knowledge and is at the heart of adult development theory.

My belief is that the acquisition of tactical knowledge does not necessarily lead to developmental growth. We all know of experts in our businesses, be they financial experts, engineering experts, marketing experts or sales experts who have an excellent grasp of their subject matter but could not be described as well developed. Perhaps the distinguishing factors at play here are intellectual intelligence versus emotional intelligence? Whatever the scientific explanation there is a distinction and understanding the difference can be critical to leaders in business in maximizing the potential of the business.

The Forfas report (mentioned above) has the following to say:
'It is clear that the theory of management and the principles of functional and commercial activities (e.g. marketing, financial management) can be successfully taught in a classroom setting. However, many critical managerial competencies or abilities such as communication skills, relationship building, decision making, and resilience, are not easily developed through lectures or consumption of written material. These less tangible, but critical managerial competences are best developed through experiential learning.'

The following are three modes of experiential learning:
- Coaching
- Mentoring
- Action learning

In recent years, coaching and mentoring have expanded at a very significant rate. See ICF Global Coaching Study 2012 here: http://coachfederation.org/coachingstudy2012/

It is evident that coaching and mentoring are widely used now across the world as developmental interventions.
Coaching and mentoring are now recognized as valuable interventions in organizational training and development.
'Coaching and mentoring are learning relationships which help people to take charge of their own development, to release their potential and to achieve results which they value'
Connor & Pokora (2007)

Mentoring

The focus of mentoring at work is on career development. Traditionally, mentoring is defined as a relationship between an older, more experienced mentor and a younger, less experienced protégé for the purpose of helping and developing the protégé's career. The primary focus of a mentoring relationship is on career development and growth.

Mentors derive great satisfaction from this work and it gives meaning and a sense of purpose. While protégés benfit from acquiring some of the wisdom of age and experience.

Coaching

Coaching as a development intervention is understood to mean facilitating growth and change over time and so coaching that is described as developmental would aim to support the coachee to make the changes necessary to grow and mature.

Coaching facilitates progress, expansion and the realisation of potential. Inherent in coaching is an expectation of movement from the level of performance of the coachee currently to where he or she wants to be, in relation to making practical changes in the work environment, making changes in response to emotional pressure or making changes in levels of understanding.

Coaching doesn't just focus on problem solving it also helps the client to built capacity to solve future problems.

Developmental coaching is seen as a recognition by the coach or manager of a persons skills and potential, and the provision of opportunities to develop or use those skills in the course of their work. Developmental coaching caN be viewed as a natural progression from skills and performance training.

Action Learning

Action Learning is based on 4 principles:
- Based on Inquiry:
  The method seeks many answers not just one. Learning is gleaned from group inquiry and reflection as different perspectives are explored.
- It is accountability focused:

Where diverse perspectives are valued turf wars and the need to have all the answers are diminished.

- Learning is systemic:

People learn together and in this environment leaders and teams develop a capacity for shared problem solving which brings about systemic change.

- Leader Centric:

The leader brings the challenge to the group and is then responsible for oversight of subsequent action

There are two types of action learning Team Coaching and Peer Coaching. In Peer Coaching individuals come together in group session to learn from each other's perspectives but have no shared accountability for action. In Team Coaching the issues, challenges and responsibility for implementation is shared.

Blocks to Development

Frequently management practices in organizations are designed to ensure that people meet agreed standards and don't slip below the required levels. Vast amounts of energy are used in ensuring that any slippage is minimized and at the same time this management effort ensures that standards above and beyond the required standard are not achieved because the pre-occupation is with ensuring an absence of deviance. While this may seem perverse it is a reality in current management practice in many organizations.

CONCLUSION

In this short article I have touched on some key elements of a best in class talent development strategy. I have given references to videos, reports and books and I encourage you to explore further. Talent development is considered as a "mission-critical" process. High performing companies see the talent development organization-wide as a necessity. They use carefully considered definitions of talent, measurable criteria and a rigorous process to determine who belongs in the talent pool and who does not.

The outcomes are measured as KPIs. Talent development strategy starts before you hire and continues throughout employment. In the words of Robert Kegan we live in an age where we all need to be 'psychologically self-employed', to know our values, our strengths and how we add value to our organizations or businesses. The challenge then is to exploit this potential and give greater meaning to our lives while adding value to the organizations and communities we work in.

Very often the biggest cost in an organization is the cost of human capital. Not leveraging best value from your investment in people deprives them and your business of an opportunity to do what is natural for us in evolutionary terms; that is to become the best we can be.

REFERENCES

Books:
Collins, J. (2004) *'Good to Great'*. USA: Random House Business Books

Connor, M. & Pokora, J. (2007) *'Coaching and mentoring at work: developing effective practice'*. England: McGraw-Hill.

Garvey Berger, J. (2012), *'Changing on the Job'*, California: Stanford University Press

Goleman D. et al (2002), *'The New Leaders'*, USA: Harvard Business School Press
Heifetz, R et al. (2009), *'The Practice of Adaptive Leadership'* USA: Harvard Business School Publishing

Reports:
Management Development Council (2010) *'Management Development in Ireland'*
http://www.forfas.ie/media/100316mdc-management-development-in-ireland.pdf

Industry Week.com (2010) *'Leadership in Manufacturing'*

http://www.industryweek.com/PrintArticle.aspx?ArticleID=2614
8&ShowAll=1&SectionID=2

Intertrade Ireland (2009) Management Matters in Northern Ireland
and Republic of Ireland
http://www.intertradeireland.com/media/intertradeirelandcom/r
esearchandstatistics/publications/tradeandbusinessdevelopment/
Management%20matters%20in%20Northern%20Ireland%20a
nd%20Republic%20of%20Ireland.pdf

Videos
Iain McGilchrist (2011) *'The Divided Brain.* UK, RSA; RSA
Animate
http://comment.rsablogs.org.uk/2011/10/24/rsa-animate-divided-
brain/

Dan Pink (2010) 'Drive'. UK: RSA; RSA Animate
http://www.youtube.com/watch?v=u6XAPnuFjJc

About the Author: *Nial is a Senior Management Executive Coach.
His diverse career background as a senior executive in Retail,
Banking, and Operations, brings issue understanding and credibility
to his clients. In 2005, Nial founded Ignite Coaching to bring a
person centered, ontological and systemic approach to his clients.
He mentors, challenges, and supports his clients through authentic
interaction as they achieve sustainable adaptive change and
personal development.*

*His clients include Financial Services Companies, Insurance
Companies, Medical Device Companies, and Technology Companies
such as HP, CISCO, Stryker, Boston Scientific, and GE Healthcare,
VHI, Irish Life, AIB, NUIG and UCD/Smurfit.*

*He has worked with Professor Robert Kegan of Harvard University
using the 'Immunity to Change' framework. This methodology
creates a path for clients to understand the subliminal beliefs that
drive their current behavior assisting them in making sustainable
behavioral change to help with goal achievement and personal
development.*

Nial holds an Advanced Management Diploma in Business and Executive Coaching from the Smurfit Business School and a Post Graduate Diploma in the Psychology of Executive coaching also from 'Smurfit' (Level 9 NFQ).

19. Glimmer: The Competitive Advantage of Learning by *Dr. Susan Harwood*

EXECUTIVE SUMMARY

The GLIMMER system is designed to Generate Learning through the Integration of Motivation, Meritocracy, Experience, and Renewal to develop the competitive advantage for businesses and individuals in today's global marketplace. Learning is a core social subsystem, which occurs throughout an organization. To leverage and expand the capabilities of employees and groups within an organization, a systems approach using the relationship between learning and work (in a cycle of continuous learning) is described in the context of the organization as a learning system.

On an **organizational level, the Glimmer architecture serves** as the toolkit of design combining social and technical subsystems to create organizations in perpetual motion generating innovation, new markets, larger market share, and rapid response to change. On the **individual level, the Glimmer architecture assists** professionals by demonstrating how to integrate their career management/ planning into their day to day actions.

INTRODUCTION

The fastest way to change an existing organization is to change the skills and knowledge of those who work there. What we know operates in tandem with what we do. If we change what know, we concurrently change what tasks and projects we can do. It doesn't require a complex change plan, a long evolutionary period, or significant down time for the productivity of our current work roles. But it does require a person having access to information, experiences, and expertise to facilitate the act of learning.

A QUICK LOOK AT SYSTEMS

In our global environment, the understanding of systems shows us how to grow and experience the inter-relationship and inter-dependence of ideas, cultures, people, business, and many other attributes, which impact our lives. These parts of our lives are feeders into our learning and understanding.

Let's look at some system examples. Our bodies are a series of biological systems; our electronics keep us interconnected through various subsystems. Our laws determine how our formal social systems are to operate while our cultures are rich in the informal elements of our social systems.

In this example of social systems, laws can be viewed as elements of an independent system and culture elements as a separate independent system. When we combine these two systems (laws and culture), we have identified the subsystems, of a fully integrated society system.

There is no escaping it, we live in a world of systems and individuals have different functions in each system that they participant in. (be it active or passive participation).

System Terms

Blanchard's system element definitions provide the consistent application of design principles in the development of any system.

- **Components** input, process, output with a variety of values
- **Attributes** characterize an item's function, size, color type
- **Relationship** is the interaction between attributes and components

Systems engineering provides us with a series of "how to" steps in developing a system that does exactly what it is designed to do. Complexity and versatility are attributes of a system, which give the component of the system meaning. It tells us how the component is operationalized in harmony with other components and other attributes.

In a system the relationship provides the links between components and attributes.

Clarifying these elements leads to consistent understanding of "how they are intended to work" in the system you are designing. This step ensures alignment, predictability and replicatable functionality of the system. Through the ongoing analysis and awareness of these elements, we can develop, grow, and modify our system be it a product, an organization, a career, or even our day-to-day life.

Socio-Technical Systems
The term Socio-Technical System (STS) has many meanings depending on the functional experts who are using the concept. Simply put, a Socio-Technical is the intersecting relationships between Social Components and Technical Components laced with Attributes. For example, social sciences (psychology, sociology, anthropology) combine with technical sciences (math, computers, physics) to create an integrated high tech business environment for a common purpose or objective.

This is a very broad set of definitions compared to the STS research of such pioneers in the field as William Passmore. The change in our lifestyles, the introduction of Social Media into our daily lives, and years of process mapping in initiatives such as Lean and DFSS have changed the frequency of our STS experiences. This increased frequency expanded our use of STS calling for expanded applications of original works. You will find a short list of Socio-Technical Researchers in the Reference section of this chapter.

The Intersection of the Social and Technical

How does a socio-technical system operate daily within an organization? In a technical subsystem of an organization, **components** (procedures, tools, engineering discipline expertise) exist at all levels of the subsystem infrastructure (projects, product development, and manufacturing) and often have concurrent functions and **attributes** (metrics, cycle times, and functionality) linked together through the **relationship** of each interaction.

In a social subsystem of an organization, **components** (people, jobs, tasks, decisions) exist at all levels of the subsystems infrastructure (projects, product development, manufacturing) and often have concurrent functions and **attributes** (metrics, behaviors, expectations) linked together through the **relationship** of each interaction (communication, problem solving).

The relationship between the components of these two subsystems is seamlessly interdependent to produce the desired outcome of the business.

NOTE: The determining factor in identifying components as either system components or subsystem components is a taxonomy question. Are you defining a stand along set of components? Then this could be an independent system. Are you defining a set of components which is interdependent with other components? Then this could be a subsystem.

For example, when a manager works for another manager, may be called on to lead a special task force, often has a series of individual contributor tasks, and serves on a variety of teams. The manager is a **component** in each activity operating through **relationships** in the interactions of each assignment according to the **attributes** required to successfully complete the assignments.

The direct overlap for both the Social System and the Technical System is in the task or work completed. The work is the same for both systems, but how the emphasis of the work differs.

Figure 19.1: Glimmer: An Organizational as a System

Glimmer: An Organization as A System
© *potencia, inc* 2002

There are two key points to observe as we examine an organization as a system: **Cause and Effect** and **Opportunities**. If you want to know what components of your organizational system are not aligned, ask your people. They know; they have most likely told you; and each day you don't fix it or explain why, you lose their confidence and trust.

Cause and Effect. Say you change the performance schedule in the performance box. Then you must also change any other box, which is impacted such as job definition, work design, reward system, budgets, and talent management.

An organization system functions optimally when there is full component alignment. Every time you alter something in one of the boxes (components) on the chart, you must look at all the other boxes (components) to determine which of these boxes must also be adjusted.

You are looking at the cause and effect relationship between the change you made to the performance schedule and expected and sometimes-unexpected changes, which must also be made to ensure continual alignment the system.

Opportunities Every box (component) has an attribute of learning and working. Everything we do in an organization has an opportunity to learn or apply learning. Productivity initiatives such as Lead Manufacturing, Design for Six Sigma, ISO, and hosts of change projects have analyzed this same chart (or one similar to it) in search of cost savings and efficiencies. That is **NOT** the objective in this analysis. We are seeking targeted investment opportunities through learning that will expand capabilities people and groups for the greatest leverage.

Sometimes that is with a select group of individuals at other times it may be by joint partnerships with universities or other companies. The more capabilities (knowledge, skills, and abilities) your people have and are utilize, the more competencies your organization can demonstrate. This seems like the appropriate place to point out that I am not referring to investments in "high potential" folks in your organization. A significant mistake being made is to focus on these individuals while the rest of the organization starves for development. If they are truly high potential, they are and will be successful in a learning organization culture.

Think of it this way, when you are walking, you are consciously doing something (the act of walking), but you are also unconsciously doing many things (breathing, heart beating) simultaneously. In most organizations, employees are consciously working and unconsciously learning simultaneously.

THE CORE FOUNDATION: Learning and Doing

Employees are often considered diamonds in the rough with many organizations. How these diamonds in the rough become the polished diamonds that develop leading edge technology, products, and services required in today's fast paced changing markets is the focus of the **Glimmer System**.. Building career skills and options for your employees leads to increased options for your organization.

As we examine these two variables: learning and work in the "Foundation Cycle of Change" model, we expand our understanding of the interdependence of these variables. To put it simply, we learn a skill, we can do a task utilizing that skill, as we do the task, we learn new aspects of the skill. The depth and breadth of these two component activities are baseline actions enabling us to build successful careers, businesses, and organizations.

Do not be fooled by the use of terms in the "Foundation Cycle of Change" model. While the words are familiar, the definitions are not the same ho-hum uses for these important life-force activities.

Figure 19.2: Foundation Cycle of Change

Glimmer: Foundation Cycle of Change
© potencia, inc 2007

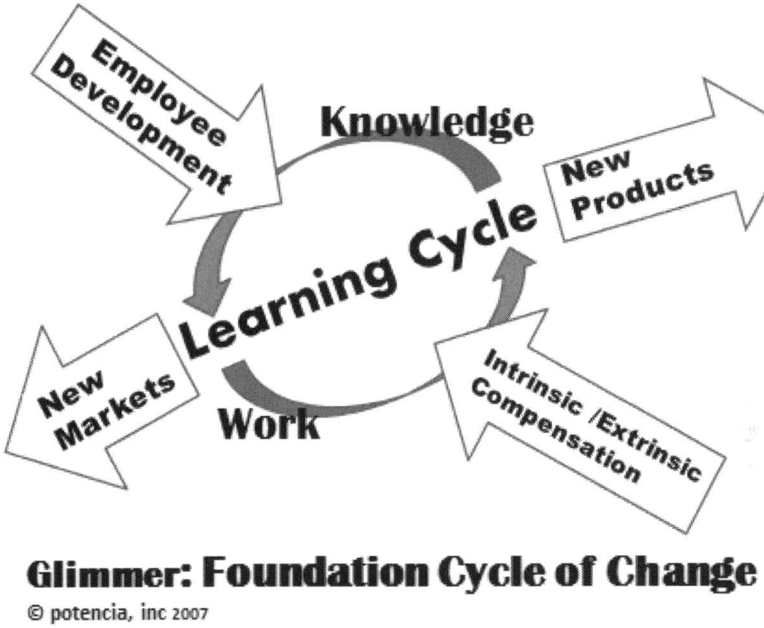

Definition of terms:

Compensation…..includes all types of intrinsic and extrinsic reward available to individuals in your organization. Historically, our focus in compensation has been only on the extrinsic of money, stock, and bonuses. These are certainly expected by employees, but they are rarely motivators for exceptional performance and thinking. If your organization is particularly generous in money and lax in performance management, you could be de-incentivizing folks by eliminating the accomplishment significance associated with the financial rewards.

Other modes of currency such as conference attendance, special project assignments, and unique recognition moments are often more aligned to a person's intrinsics or passions. There is a cart and horse issue here. Before you can design intrinsic rewards, you first must know your employees well enough to be aware of what would fit into this category for them.

Career planning holds a parallel cart and horse opportunity for individuals. What are your intrinsic motivators? How do you use them in your career today? How do you see them influencing your choices? These are some of the initial questions asked in the self-awareness portion of the **Glimmer Career Planning toolkit**.

Employee Development.... encompasses a sea of possibilities. An employee is a multifaceted complex asset. Think of your employee as an iceberg. What you see above the surface is a very small fraction of the skills and abilities invisible under the surface.

The challenge in today's employee development actions is to make more of the invisible, visible and optimal. If we only think of the current work the employee is doing, we will not be prepared for the emerging knowledge we need our employees to have. One of the "aha" moments created during skill road mapping projects is the skill acceleration in both need and employee readiness that occurs as a result of the process and awareness on the part of employees.

Creating robust employee development options far exceeds the traditional "butts in seats training approach" to knowledge and skill building. Many organizations, managers, and employees continue to believe that an employee sitting in passive mode, either in a classroom or in front of a computer screen is creating leading edge learning, thinking, or skills. Why? Is that how you built your skills? Most likely, your skill building is and has been an on-going combination of self-study, trial and error, mentoring, listening, exploring, and the occasional workshop. This is also the approach Glimmer helps you create in your individual career development awareness.

New Markets.... are output examples of the Learning Cycle. There are two types of new markets for us to explore. The customer group who has never seen or utilized your existing products or services is the traditional and viable place to expand your market. Timing and the cost of expansion are two of the considerations firms consider when making these decisions. The learning cycle generates the analysis, alternatives, and scenarios to ensure the success of these expansions.

The new customer for the new product is straight forward step in the product introduction cycle. The value added by the learning cycle provides is creativity strategy and execution innovation to enter these markets and capture the new customer. The new customer for a new use of an existing technology is another aspect to the new market definition. My favorite example of this concept to date is the Wii technology. A brilliant extended use of old technology with upgraded packaging, software, and appeal to a wide customer base.

New Products.....are exciting to use, thrilling to develop, and a result of hundreds of learning cycles in action. The origination of new products is the minds and passions of the developers supported by the learning cycles of each functional department and employee who nurtures the new product from concept through to the hands of the customer.

Note: How this innovation occurs is covered in more depth in the GLIDE: Innovation is a Choice chapter 13 of this book.

Figure 19.3 provides a visual example of where the hundreds of learning cycles are generated each day in our organizations.

Figure 19.3: Glimmer: Learning Organization Components

Glimmer: Learning Organization Components
© potencia, inc 2002

Applying organizational systems solutions to your career

Well, all that sounds great, but how does that help me and my career? I don't work for a big company and I don't have the luxury of those big budgets. Gosh, I thought you'd never ask. Your career is your responsibility regardless of where you work. The next figure captures career development options for individuals.

The question asked repeatedly of every child is "**what do you want to be when you grow up**?" You have thought about this, worried about it, sought counseling about it, discussed this with all your friends and most of your family. Some folks have invested thousands of dollars and years of your lives in colleges and universities seeking this answer. Me too!

Until you know you; no one can help you find your career. They can share their experience, that's valuable. They can tell you what they have observed are your strong points, that's valuable. They can even tell you, "If I were you, this is what I would do" again, helpful, but not the answer.

Figure 19.4: Glimmer: Career Development Elements

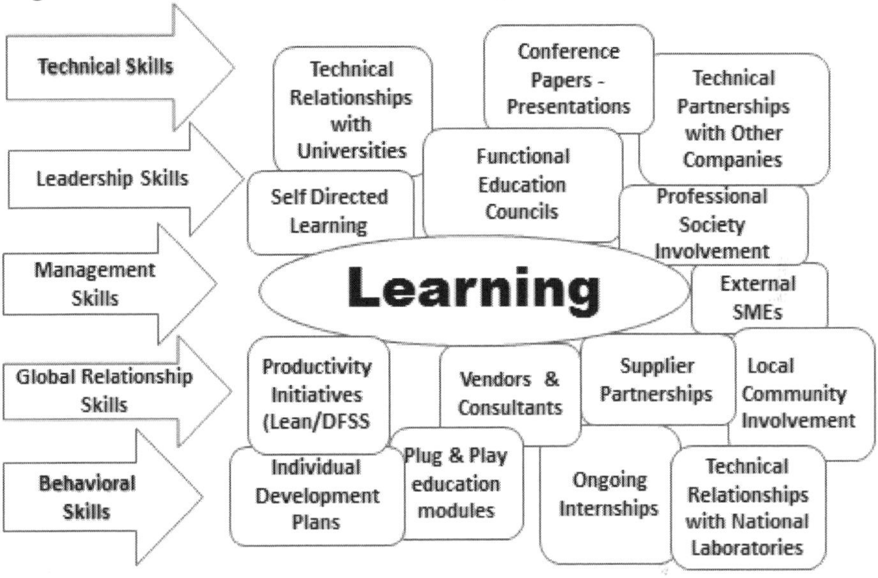

Glimmer: Career Development Elements
© potencia, inc. 2006

Exploring Self Exercise: The first step in launching your career development activity is to make a list of how you spend your time each day; What type of things do you like to do? What do you do well? What could you use a bit of improvement in? Honesty and clarity with yourself as to who you are, what you are passionate about, and how much effort are you willing to invest are all essential information points as you begin.

Once you have these insights about you, the Glimmer career development elements can help you frame your next steps. Customize this to be meaningful for you.

If what you love isn't on the chart......add it. Reinvent yourself to what you want to be and do from where you are today.

CONCLUSION

The **GLIMMER** system is a fresh approach to learning optimization for both organizations and individuals with today's global skill market demand in mind. The ability to customize components of the architecture enables professionals and organizations to quickly transition in the ever shifting market demand using an effective transaction series of tools and techniques while achieving the goal of sustainable competitive advantage

PostScript: As unique as the Glimmer system is, the structure of the book is equally unique. Have you ever purchased a book and found that you only needed 2 or 3 chapters of the book? I have, so I designed the **GLIMMER** book as a **toolbox** to enable you to customize your book based on what you tools you need. There are 7 chapters in the **GLIMMER** book / **toolbox**: The Overview Chapter and 6 "How To" chapters enabling you to customize your **GLIMMER** system. You only purchase what you need to guide your career and/or organization to optimal competitive advantage. Release date: Spring 2013 (www.glimmeronline.com)

REFERENCES

Avgerou,C. Ciborra,C.,and Land, F.F, editors (2004) The Social Study of Information and Communication Technology: Innovation, Actors and Context Oxford, OUP
Blanchard,B and Fabrycky,W, (2010) Systems Engineering and Analysis, Fifth Edition, Prentice Hall, 2010
Kossiakoff, A and Sweet, W, (2003) Systems Engineering Principles and Practice. Wiley-Interscience, .
Passmore, W (1988) Designing Effective Organizations: The Sociotechnical Systems Perspective, John Wiley & Sons.
http://www.sociotechical.org/archive.htm
http://www.sociotechnical.org
http://essex ac.uk/chimera

*About the Author: Susan is an energizing professional who transform business, leadership, and organizations. Through her firm, **Potencia, Inc**. founded in 2000 (www.potenciaconsulting.com), she develops innovative solutions through her unique blend of strong academic credentials; successful global business experience; international entrepreneurial research projects, and clarity of purpose. Hundreds of Fortune 500 and National Laboratory leaders have been developed through her leadership academies and personal coaching.*

*Katzenback's book, **The Wisdom of Teams**, the London Times, and the Human Resources Executive have written of her system's approach to organizational design and learning. Clients include, new venture start-ups, Lockheed, DOE, Telespazio, Los Alamos National Laboratory, Medtronic, IMTI, and Motorola. She is described as "intellectually-agile, visionary, passionate, articulate, astute, and action oriented". As a captivating speaker and facilitator, Susan inspires and challenges individuals to unleash the power of their potential.*

*As Project Manager for the Irish Executive Press, she lead the integration of 14 leading practitioners' contributions to create **Best Practices for Success Business** available at www.irishexecutive.com. Currently, she is completing 3 publication projects: **New Life Lifestyles: Rethinking how we live** www.newlifestyles.me) release date fall 2012; **GLIDE: Unleashing the Innovation within** with co-author Dr. Eric Maass, (www.glideonline.co); and **GLIMMER: Creating Competitive Advantage through Learning** , (www.glimmeronline.com), release dates Spring 2013.*

Susan's credentials include: PhD and MA, Fielding Graduate University specializing in the Psychology of Leadership; a MGA specializing in Organizational Processes, University of Maryland, European Division; and a BS in Technical Education, University of Akron.

20. Leveraging Cultural Diversity by *Patricia Ryall*

EXECUTIVE SUMMARY

The need for labor and skills to support Ireland's boom during the Celtic tiger years resulted in an unprecedented influx of immigrant workers. The proportion of the population born outside the Republic of Ireland more than doubled during the late 90's and early years of the 21st century. Though our economy is longer booming, these new Irish citizens have since settled and are here to stay. The rapid shift from a predominantly indigenous and homogenous workforce to a culturally diverse one brings challenges and opportunities for Irish organizations. In order to fully reap the potential benefits of this new cultural diversity, its effective management is of long term interest to businesses and organizations in Ireland. This paper seeks to discuss how cultural diversity may be managed and leveraged for positive effect both for the culturally diverse workforce and the organization competing in an increasingly globalized economy.

INTRODUCTION

People have been aware of other cultures since the time of Columbus's explorations in the 13th century and before. However this awareness has been amplified in the 21st century as globalization continues to accelerate and developments in technology and social media effectively transcend global geography. While the 21st century world is shrinking, the business opportunities and challenges these changes pose are expanding day on day. One of the most significant global business challenges is the effective management of cultural diversity.

Here in Ireland our population remained relatively homogenous until the middle '90's. However the boom of the Celtic tiger years dramatically changed our cultural mix with the influx of immigrants to service our labor shortage. Consequently the proportion of population born outside of the republic of Ireland more than doubled in 10 years between '96 and '06.(1) Though the boom years have become a distant memory, our cultural mix is here to stay and we continue to work and share Irish society with people from different cultures on a daily basis.

So what is Culture? Simply put Culture comprises the values, beliefs and behaviors shared by a group of people whether they are of different nationality, religion, geography, language or workplace. However nationality and the nation state are most closely associated with culture though the nation state it in itself can encompass many cultures.

While a cultural mix offers business many opportunities as well as challenge, the ability to cash in on these offerings depends to a large degree on how effectively or poorly we communicate with business partners in or from a different cultural setting to ours. Simply put they are different and we need to take this difference into account to collaborate with other individuals from other cultures and manage and leverage cultural diversity effectively. Organizations need to mindfully create an organizational learning environment that is open, flexible and respectful of cultural difference.

The use of well proven cultural training models underpinned by a coaching approach has historically proved very effective in creating such an environment. Training models available are all or mostly based on the work of Geert Hofstede, interculturalist, and key figure in this area. Hotstede began researching cross-cultural groups and organizations in the 60's and his findings have played a major role in developing a systematic framework for assessing and differentiating national cultures and organizational cultures.

He initially undertook research into national culture differences across subsidiaries of a multinational corporation (IBM) in 64 countries. Subsequent studies by others covered students in 23 countries, elites in 19 countries, commercial airline pilots in 23 countries, up-market consumers in 15 countries, and civil service managers in 14 countries. Together these studies identified and validated four independent dimensions of national culture differences. A fifth dimension, 'long term orientation' was added in 1991 and a sixth 'indulgence versus restraint' in 2010. Kluckhohn and Fred Strodtbeck, Edward Hall and Fons Trompenaars and more recently Rosinsky in 2004 have all produced training models which are loosely based on the original by Hofstede.

These models generally set out to distinguish cultures from each other through a framework of cultural dimensions. Different cultures are placed on a continuum within the dimensions depending on preferences and cultural inclination.

Strategically managing cultural diversity by putting in an effective training and coaching program based on the latter reaps many rewards. Not only will staff feel more valued but a successfully managed multicultural workplace creates opportunity for learning, creativity, innovation and leadership in the workforce by bringing different perspectives and experiences to the organisation. Though Ireland in the noughties is no longer booming and our requirements are changed, our country's cultural diversity is here to stay.

This cultural mix can positively impact on business bottom line and social integration if managed appropriately and well. Strategic diversity management gives Ireland the potential to be among the most innovative and dynamic places to work in the world and our organisations leaders in the field of cross cultural competence.

"Your individuality is the most valuable thing you have." Martha Beck

"*The real voyage of discovery consists not in seeking new landscapes but in having new eyes.*" Marcel Prous

Background
As technological advance and social media growth continue to shrink our world, globalization (a buzzword coined in the early 90s referring to the influence and the convergence of world financial markets) has become a ubiquitous term. Ireland like many other countries has to compete on a global stage and we have Irish and multinational companies based in Ireland, whose employees interact daily with colleagues of different cultures. Moreover the Celtic tiger made a significant dent on Ireland's cultural mix with the influx of immigrant workers to feed our booming economy. (1) We went from predominantly indigenous and homogenous workforce in the mid-

90s, to a diverse cultural mix including Africans and Asians but primarily immigrants from central Europe during the Celtic tiger years.

In 2009 just over a quarter of non-Irish national's resident here were UK nationals and two thirds were from the EU. While the absolute numbers have grown significantly the percentage of non-Irish nationals from other regions is low Asia (11%), Africa (8%) and the Americas (5%).In 2009 just over a quarter of non-Irish nationals resident here are UK nationals and 2 third were from EU (CSO: Population and Migration Estimates 2003 and 2006) (2)

Though the boom is over, organisations continue to grapple with the challenges of cultural diversity in the workforce. These range from basic communication and language difficulties to more complex issues around decision making and team processes. Yet the United States and other multicultural economies have demonstrated that it is not only possible to effectively manage cultural difference but it's possible to leverage cultural diversity for greater organisational learning, creativity, innovation and leadership.

This paper examines the models, principles and benefits of a strategic approach to cultural diversity management.

Culture as context in the Globalized Workplace
However before we examine the impact of culture in the workplace we need to address the concept of Culture. One definition suggests that 'Culture consists in patterned ways of thinking, feeling and reacting, acquired and transmitted mainly by symbols, constituting the distinct achievements of human groups, including their embodiments in artifacts; the essential core of culture consists of traditional (i.e. historically derived and selected) ideas and especially their attached values' (Kluckhohn cited in Hofstede, 2001)

Hofstede interculturalist and key figure in this area condenses the above definition by describing culture as 'the collective programming of the mind that distinguishes members of one group or category of people from another' (Hofstede, 2001).

He sees culture as a core system of values which are invisible but outwardly manifest by layers of practice; rituals, heroes and symbols (Figure 20.1). Rituals are collective activities, not necessarily essential are deemed important to keep individuals within the norms of society e.g. business protocols. Heroes are people alive, dead or part of a myth that possess highly valued characteristics and serve as valuable role models in society and symbols represent the most superficial layer of cultural practices and comprise of things such as gestures, pictures, dress code or fashion.

Figure 20.1: Hofstede's Onion Diagram: Manifestation of Culture at Different Levels (Hofstede, 2001)

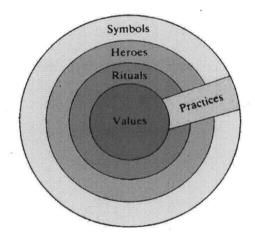

While many cultural definitions exist, attempts to define culture generally speak of the values, beliefs and behaviors shared by a group of people where group refers to nationality, religion, workplace or profession etc. Organizations also have their own distinct cultures based on the shared values, assumptions and learning.

Probably the most common notion of culture is that of nation state and geography but this can also be complex e.g., people in a particular social grouping in their own country i.e. fashion designers may have more in common with fashion designers in a different country than with their own countrymen!

In 1980, Hofstede, a pioneer in this field, was one of the first interculturalists to isolate aspects of culture which are specifically relevant to the workplace by creating a model that initially identified four distinct dimensions based on the common tendencies of people. With a fifth dimension, long term orientation (LTO) initially called Confucian dynamism added in 1991 and a sixth, indulgence versus restraint, in 2010. Cultures or nations are placed on the continuum according to cultural preference/orientation.

Table 20.a: Hofstede's 5 dimensions

1. *Power Distance* – the extent to which the less powerful person in a society accepts inequality in power and considers it normal
2. *Uncertainty Avoidance* – the extent to which people feel nervous in a situation they consider to be unstructured, unclear or unpredictable
3. *Individualism –Collectivism* – the extent to which individuals look after their own interests or those of the group to which they belong and are loyal and which looks after them- extended family, organisation etc.
4. *Masculinity-Femininity* – masculine cultures define very distinct social roles for men and women. Men are expected to be assertive, competitive, strong, fast and materialistic.
5. *Long/Short-term Orientation* – the extent to which people focus their efforts on the present or future

Of the five dimensions identified by Hofstede, each one had at least one if not more cultural continuums. However this is only one of numerous models that exist to specially manage culture difference in the workplace. Since then other experts, including Florence Kluckhohn and Fred Strodtbeck, Edward Hall and Fons Trompenaars have created various cultural diversity models based on Hofstede's work adding additional updates/approaches per research results. In 2004 Philippe Rosinski created the Cultural Orientations Framework **(COF) which is an integrative framework designed to assess and compare cultures.**

A CULTURAL ORIENTATION according to Rosinski 'is an inclination to think, feel or act in a way that is culturally determined.

For example, in the United States, people tend to communicate in a direct fashion, saying what they mean, and meaning what they say. The message is clear, but it can also be perceived as offensive. Their cultural orientation, then, is "direct communication," in contrast with Asians' typical indirectness. Asians don't necessarily spell out what they mean, at the risk of being misunderstood, because they wish to avoid hurting someone's feelings'.

The COF includes a range of cultural dimensions/orientations grouped in seven categories including sense of power and responsibility, time management approaches, definitions of identity and purpose, organizational arrangements, notions of territory and boundaries, communication patterns, and modes of thinking.

Managing Cultural diversity- a strategic approach

As we can see models may be a useful means of creating vision and developing a strategy which is comprehensive, coordinated, purposeful and integrated with other organizational strategies. However regardless of the cultural diversity model used, the principle of empathetic honest communication underpins the value of any successful framework in managing cultural variations. 'Understanding communication processes and developing a means of managing effective communication while remaining open and flexible in the workplace are integral to successful diversity management (Henderson 1994)

Ultimately, it is through communication verbal and nonverbal that we relate to one another and understand and overcome our differences (Touraine, 2000). Effective programs that reap rewards, seek to recognize and celebrate difference, and do not try to assimilate individuals or encourage everyone to fit institutional values and beliefs of the majority. Instead the approach emphasizes valuing the individual and encouraging them to draw on their own values and beliefs for problem solving and decision making (McMillan-Capehart, 2006; Thomas and Ely, 1996).

Coaching approach

As Culture is complex and not one dimensional, the addition of coaching to a diversity training programme can make a unique contribution in consolidating its underlying guiding principles i.e. communication, openness and flexibility. Coaching is also underpinned by these principles and seeks to create increased awareness and responsibility in the person being coached. If cross cultural coaching is part of a diversity programme in the organisation, the people and organisation will slowly learn and change to create the ideal conditions for sustained cross cultural success.

Good coaching improves people's awareness of their own cultural perspectives. The critical first step in any cross cultural awareness program; it also seeks to create greater responsibility and leadership in the coachee. There is no 'we are doing it to them stuff'; learning is a two-way process and 'we have as much to learn from the outsider as they have from us'. The coachee is not passively learning lists of cultural traits but working at a more fundamental level to improve his communication and interpersonal skills. Cultural diversity may be personally challenging for the individual also the organization because fundamental changes in people and company culture may be required. However mutually respectful exchange coupled with genuine interest can do wonders to create trust and bring down intercultural barriers.

The coachee learns how to be present, to participate in the moment with people that are different and stay flexible about difference. He aims to overcome differences not by eliminating them but by acknowledging them and finding ways to make the most of them. People become more open to learning and open to expressing where they may have difficulties. Humour is also useful; taking outcomes seriously but not taking yourself seriously brings ease and tolerance into conversation. This openness and flexibility is personally challenging as there is an element of unpredictability so coaching can act as a useful support when development and change is taking place. Learning to ask open questions and listen respectfully as part of the process naturally creates conditions for a good conversation regardless of cultural background.

Organizational requirements
In a sense while everyone is the organization is leading the way to a

more open, flexible creative environment, it requires a commitment from the top to manage the challenges that the cultural diversity program asks of everyone in the organization.

Thomas and Ely (1996) discovered that certain organizational preconditions enabled organizations to use cultural differences for learning, growth and renewal. Firstly leaders must appreciate and be tolerant of different perspective and approaches to work, and truly value variety of opinion and insight.

(This may be challenging at first as it may be contrary to some management styles; a coaching program is ideal in this situation to identify and address any issues) Organizations must create an expectation of high standards. It must value personal development and openness and have a relatively egalitarian, non-bureaucratic structure. Finally it must have a well-articulated and widely understood mission.

The basic concept of managing diversity accepts that a workforce consists of a diverse population of people. The diversity consists of visible and non-visible differences which will include factors such as sex, age, background, race, disability, personality and work style. It is founded on the premise that harnessing these differences will create a productive environment in which everyone feels values, where their talents are being fully utilized and in which organizational goals are met.' (Kandola and Fullerton. 1994).

So while training models are very useful pointers, it's at the very least naïve and at the worse detrimental to hold on to these models as the sole map or the way forward, it's down to us to create fundamental change by becoming more self-aware and responsible in a cross cultural situation. To work well in cross cultural situation is to have a "beginner's mind"every day!

What is important is not what the organizations culture is but whether it is open to progressive diversity management with open communication and whether it has the flexibility to learn and adapt (Henderson, 1994; Hobman, et al., 2004; Kandola and Fullerton, 1994).

Why you might use a diversity model

According to Rodriguez (2006) the main driver for a strategic approach to diversity management is the need to tap into the creative, cultural and communicative skills of employees in order to improve policies, products and customer experience. This illustrates that the basis for a business case it to improve business performance. Internationally world class companies such as IBM, PepsiCo, HP, KLM, and Volvo all have strategic diversity programs in place to capture the widest variety of cultural skills. The following is a list of benefits underpinning the above argument:

- o Increase creativity and innovation in workforce by bringing difference perspectives and experiences to the organisation
- o Business negotiations, marketing, sales and purchasing are all facilitated by through knowledge and understanding of cultural differences
- o Higher staff retention of non-national employees as they experience greater job satisfaction
- o Increased productivity, lower levels of absenteeism and staff turnover
- o Attract more talent as emphasis on individual socialisation in the cultural diversity programmes lead to overall workforce feeling more appreciated and valued (McMillan-Capehart, 2006).

CONCLUSION

- o The multicultural organisation is here to stay. It's not about tolerating or eliminating cultural differences but proactively acknowledging them; honestly listening and engaging with other cultures in an open flexible and respectful manner drawing on the humanistic principles of good communication. In this way we create enhanced methods of intercommunication and greater multicultural cohesion.
- o Cultural Diversity management requires strong leadership and a coordinated and strategic approach. It cannot rely on adhoc interventions when problems have already occurred. Cultural diversity programmes demand courage in challenging the individual to become aware of his cultural beliefs/prejudices. He is asked to let go and open to new possibilities and perspectives of being and doing for the

benefit of all. Humor, creativity and a willingness to be wrong are all necessary ingredients!

- o It will take time and effort and a willingness to learn and change both for individuals and the organization
- o Culture is a complex and dynamic phenomena that cannot be simply reduced to lists of behaviors and while it can be tempting to rely on generalizations, this often leads to misleading stereotyping and frustrating intercultural communication.
- o We are asked to *adapt to* but not necessarily *adopt* other cultural points of view; our individuality and sense of uniqueness is not threatened by become cross culturally competent
- o No matter what future economic changes take place in Ireland, the impact of our recent experience will persist and cultural diversity will ripple through future generations. As a nation if we learn from others and get it right from the beginning, our organist ions are well placed to become leaders in cultural diversity management thereby enhancing our position in an increasingly multicultural global marketplace.

REFERENCES

1. CSO: Census of Population Data, 2006

2. CSO: Population and Migration Estimates 2003 and 2006

Hofstede, G., (2001), **Culture's Consequences**, Sage, Thousand Oaks.

Rosinski, P., (2003), **COACHING ACROSS CULTURES**, Nicholas Brealey Publishing.

Rosinski, P., www.CoachingAcrossCultures.com

Henderson, G., (1994), **Cultural Diversity in the workplace: Issues and Strategies**, Praeger Westport, CT.

Touraine, A., (2000), **Can we live together? Equality and difference**, Stanford University Press, Stanford.

McMillan-Capehart, A., (2006), **Heterogeneity or Homogeneity: Socialization makes the difference in firm performance**, Performance Improvement Quarterly, Vol. 19 No.1, 83.

Thomas, D.A., and Ely, R.J., (1996), **Making Differences Matter**, Harvard Business Review, Vol. 74, No. 5, 79-90.

Kandola, R., and Fullerton, J., (1994), **Managing the mosaic: Diversity in Action**, Institute of Personal Development, London.
Hobman, E.V., et Al. (2004), **Perceived Dissimilarity and work group involvement : the moderating effects of group openness to diversity**, Group and Organization Management, Vol. 29, No. 5,560-588

Rodriguez, R., (2006), **Diversity finds its place,** HR Magazine vol. 51, No. 8.

About the Author: *Patricia is a seasoned Executive Coach and Business owner. Her firm offers Cross Cultural Coaching, Training Solutions, and Executive Coaching for corporate leadership and change management since 2004, drawing on her considerable experience of living and working in Asia, Australia and the United States.*

Her clients include Pharmaceutical, IT, and Relocation companies. She has also worked with the Irish public service including the Health Service Executive and The Institute of Public Administration.

She is a founding member of International Coaching Federation (ICF) Irish Chapter; an accredited member of the International Coaching Federation, and a member of the Society for Intercultural Education Training and Research (SIETAR)

Patricia holds a Bachelor Degree in Education, and is a graduate of The Coaches Training Institute, USA and UCD Michael Smurfit Graduate Business School, Dublin

21. Closing the gaps in employee engagement by *Imelda McGrattan*

INTRODUCTION

In Africa there is a saying: If you want to go quickly, go alone; If you want to go far, go with a group. Business is made up of groups of people working collectively to achieve results.

In order to optimise a business' efficiency and effectiveness it is of the utmost importance that people are consistently engaged on their own individual level with the current business practices and technology that will support growth.

Employees make you money, lose you money and all the time they are costing you money. They are either a valuable asset or a drain on your resources. As a business owner you may undervalue the employees that have been hired due to time constraints on getting to know and understand how each individual can work more effectively to achieve goals.

It is all too easy to assume that employees have understood what the business requirements are just because they performed well at interview, training induction was provided and a Handbook of Employee Terms & Conditions was issued before you leave them off to get on with the job. If everyone within your business is working to the minimum requirement, it just isn't enough in today's competitive environment!

Looking to the future will require employers to proactively move away from controlling their employees to enabling them. Outdated, outmoded tools that create inefficiencies will have to be replaced. Change will become the normal concept and how each individual business adapts to it will become part of their branding and their customer's perception.

So how do we really engage people and make them feel special, creating "ripple effects" in the day to day operational functions to ensure the job they were hired to do today, will lead to steady inspiration and effort to do the job that needs done tomorrow, before the decision is made to retire from the current position because the life expectancy for productivity is expiring.

In order to understand the significant shift that has contributed to the widening gap in employee engagement we need to look at how Technology has impacted our social interaction skills, the soft skills that are critically required today more than ever in order to get messages out, feedback in and interactions kept alive and relative to each business's overall bottom line.

TECHNOLOGY

Most businesses today will utilize technology to varying degrees in order to simplify and automate processes, run analytics on key metrics in order to compare and contrast performance and peaks and troughs in the business day / week, advertise, market and communicate with their customer base on various social media platforms. The cost benefits are relative to each business and the ROI for some of these activities is not always easy to monetise.

Technology has had a huge impact on social interactions. Information overload and short attention span windows have almost re-programmed some of our behaviours in how we communicate with people because we believe that speed is of the essence and we don't have enough time to take the time. Subject matters have become condensed into snippets of information and sound bites. Managers are under increasing pressure to hit the numbers and to explain in metrics if they fall short of expectation.

Technology should always be utilized to supplement core business activities to make the working life simpler, access data, identify trends and bottle necks, and anticipate change and risks. It is amazing the difference it can make to a business that utilizes it effectively.

The important aspect to always acknowledge is that the systems are used to support the work the employees do. Frequently though it appears that a percentage of employees have turned into some kind of robotic scripted add on to compliment the system.

Let's imagine for a minute that by consistently improving social interactive skills it is possible to address the imbalance and managers / coaches can reduce gaps in employee engagement leading to improved efficiency, drive results, and create hassle free workplaces that give you a better return on your time and employee investments helping to balance the input V output. All that is needed to start is a simple tool, a SWOT analysis to support this initial engagement to create new interactive behaviours between managers and teams creating a new awareness as to how and why employees think and operate in the manner in which they do and to implement action plans to enhance the core activities that will have the most beneficial impact on making a business a better success.

SWOT ANALYSIS PROCESS
A SWOT Analysis is very valuable business tool to utilise in identifying and comparing and contrasting how your business currently performs in relation to other competitors. The analysis process contains four easy to follow steps:

1. Using a template or sheet of paper it is possible to sit down with your team and list the Strengths, Weaknesses, Opportunities, and Threats that are within your own business world.
2. Select a benchmark competitor; list the Strengths, Weaknesses, Opportunities, and Threats of the competitor. Often this requires a bit of research. Reading the public literature and their website can give you much of the information needed for this step of the process.
3. Compare and analyse the two lists of Strengths, Weaknesses, Opportunities and Threads. How do you compare? Where are they strong you are week and vice versa. The discussion during this step is essential in gaining a more thorough knowledge of both businesses (yours and theirs).
4. Create a list of critical issues and associated actions to close any gaps between your firm and the competitor where they

are ahead of you. You may also want to develop a few actions around your strengths to ensure you stay ahead of the game.

SWOT is an excellent method if used regularly to track your progress in tracking your performance to the actions you identified. . SWOT discussions help your staff stay involved, informed and focused on the business needs remembering that value is relative to each individual and cash flow is imperative to stay afloat. More details on how to accomplish this are in the next section of this article.

Figure 21.1: Swot Analysis Work Sheet

S.W.O.T Analysis

Mgr / Coach		Date	
Team player		Review Date	
STRENGTHS: Work To Them			
WEAKNESSES: Work On Them			
OPPORTUNITIES: Make The Most Of Them			
THREATS: Overcome Them			
Action Plan			

Irish Executive Press

Actions Taken		
REVIEW: **RESULTS**		

The worksheet in Figure 21.1 can be very easily utilised to help close gaps in employee engagement enabling the managers / coaches to diary minimally a weekly / fortnightly date taking 30 minutes with each employee to listen, discuss, analyse and plan how each can help the other understand how their contribution to the overall success of the business on a daily basis can never be underestimated or taken for granted.

There are many ways to use the form. The employee can fill it out first before the initial meeting takes place doing a SWOT on their own performance and development needs in relation to the business objectives. This enables the manager to listen and note how the employee views themselves within the business and offer constructive feedback in how the work that is being carried out is contributing to the overall success of the business. The manager is able to identify the number of employees who need specific training therefore planning more appropriate cost effective training programmes to enhance skills or if possible to allocate employees work better suited to their skill base.

The manager / coach can prepare a SWOT based on the business alone, in order for both parties to discuss so the employee is always fully aware of the objectives that need to be achieved and any changes that they need to be made aware of. They discuss the strengths the business and employee have and how to build on them.

The weaknesses which can be improved upon and how integral the employee's input to this area is valued by the business, remembering that your employees may be one of the business's weaknesses.

The opportunities section allows for input in regards to new ideas, new ways of doing things and how the business can be improved. This opens the communications channels for diverse ideas to be collated, acknowledged and actioned if deemed worthy, becoming part of the recognition and reward scheme to build better employee relations. It also enables the manager to offer appropriate opportunities to the right people when they arise.

Threats and worries are discussed both internal and external enabling open, honest communication between both parties. This enables the manager to build trust, help employees believe in themselves and the information the company provides always maintaining a dignified business like confidentiality and offering the services of other parties when the issues that maybe disclosed are outside of your business remit. (E.g. personal / family / medical issues)

CLOSING THE GAPS

With the information that is collated on the form, the manager and employee are able to draft together an appropriate Action plan for the coming time period. The employee can note the actions taken, the effects they have made and inform the manager if need be before the next scheduled meeting of any concerns that have arisen. Together they can review the results at the next meeting and discuss the pertinent details that will lead to more continuous improvement for the employee and the business as a whole. In these interactions, new habits are being created; new ways of communicating and it may take time for some people to become familiar and comfortable with the process. Build the process into your business and let it become routine but never systematic!

A business that fails to include a communications training plan for its employees will deal with the negative fallout on many levels. HR recruits the employee for the job that needs done today, management's responsibility is to identify the training needs of each employee to bring out the best in them for the job that needs done tomorrow. Employees are the most valuable asset in your business if you take the time to engage with them, learn from them and give them the autonomy to make their job role a success. Remaining open-minded to their diverse input may enable you to build a business beyond your wildest dreams.

It's good to talk, they say. I say it is better to talk as little as possible but as much as necessary while listening is critical! Communication in business is over rated if the desired actions are not visible. What we say and how we say it in order to engage employees is important. Never underestimate the power of body language when delivering a message. The no.1 factor here is to limit as much resistance from the listener as possible. Keep communications professional, informative, relevant and interactive, not forgetting that a healthy sense of humour goes a long way in lifting the toughest of days.

CONCLUSION

Start today, use the SWOT! And learn to enjoy engaging with the most valuable resource your business has – its people. Cultivate a genuine interest in what they do for the business, how they do it and why they do it in the manner that it is done. Each person's motivation at work is different and can change dependent on external and internal influences. It is easy to identify people who are happy at work and the more of them you have, the better the odds are of your business surviving and thriving.

About the Author*: Imelda McGrattan teaches and mentors people how to create more effective business relationships and generate short term through long term goals for completive advantage in local and global marketplace.*
As a freelance consultant, her experience in the sales environment, education, retail, telecommunications, transport, financial, hospitality and the warehousing & logistics industry supply chain provide a unique integrated perspective to clients.
A no nonsense diplomatic style with people enables her quickly scope a firm's issues, develop an improvement plan and help to implement successful strategies simply in a cost effective approach

22. Executive Job Hunting by *Ken McIntyre-Barn*

EXECUTIVE SUMMARY

Career transition at senior level is difficult as there are fewer opportunities and plenty of tough competition. I say to many people and many people say to me "Looking for a job is a full time job"-you get back what you put in. Your success will depend on the amount of time and effort you put into the correct activities to secure that dream job.

The Successful Executive Job Hunting chapter in the Irish Executives Book on Best Practice for Business Success will provide you with valuable advice to enhance your job search campaign and improve your competitiveness. If you embrace this journey with a positive attitude and openness to meeting new people and helping others you will find it rewarding and fulfilling.

INTRODUCTION

Career transition at senior level is becoming more difficult as there are fewer opportunities and plenty of tough competition. More and more executives are using career coaches to improve their competitiveness, marketability and ultimately the success of their job search campaign. Although each individual's circumstances are different there are many commonalities to an effective job search.

Before you do anything - ensure you have a strong, positive and energetic attitude. If you are unhappy in your job or unemployed it can be demoralizing and depressing. If you appear uncomfortable, stressed, desperate or anxious, the people you meet will spot this quickly.

A successful job campaign covers multiple areas across three distinct phases:
1. Planning and Preparation
2. Go to Market
3. Closing the deal / On-Boarding.

Phase One - Planning and Preparation

A former boss once told me; 90% preparation = 10% perspiration, 10% preparation = 90% perspiration. Don't underestimate the importance of building the correct foundations for your job search campaign. The time and effort you invest in this phase will save you time in the long term and make your job search more effective. The key stages in this phase are:

1. Skills and competency assessment

It is essential for each individual to be fully aware of the skills and expertise that they can bring to an organization. There are various methods to identify these ranging from psychometric assessments, self-assessment questionnaires, reviewing achievements right through to reviewing previous appraisals. Never claim to be what you are not. If you cannot easily give an example of a strength or competency you may need to review whether this really is a key strength. Recruitment processes have become more rigorous and the use of competency based interviewing is more commonplace so inaccurate claims about strengths and expertise will be found out!

2. CV / Resume preparation

Remember the CV / Resume is to get the interview, not the job and yet so many people misunderstand this and set about trying to communicate every element of their career on their CV. What many people fail to understand is that the small amount of time initially given to reading a CV at the initial screening stage to determine if the CV contains the "must haves" described in the job description or assignment brief. In large recruitment firms this is sometimes done by a "sifter" which further raises the importance of ensuring your CV includes key information.

A good CV usually starts with a profile / career summary which is essentially your elevator pitch. Ideally each section of your CV should be interesting and compelling enough to encourage the reader to continue reading. Never assume that people will know the company you work for so always include 1-2 lines to describe each company you have worked with e.g. €x billion consumer product manufacturer operating in x countries globally with over x thousand employees.

Although it is important to describe your position never just cut and paste your job description into your CV. Include important aspects such as the size of team you manage, turnover, profit and budgetary responsibilities and remember to include achievements. As a guide include 1-2 achievements per year for each position.

3. Cover letters

Although an essential accompaniment for job applications, in many cases cover letters are never read. Remember "less is more" - a cover letter should not be longer than ¾ page - anything more is too long to read. Develop a suite of cover letters which can be edited and used quickly at short notice e.g. prospective employers, responses to advertisements, executive recruiters. Ideally your letter should contain three key areas:

- An introduction requesting your consideration for a particular position within a company.
- Highlight your expertise. In many cases this will be tailored depending on the company and position you are applying for and what the company is actually looking for.
- Close the sale: Include some reference to the fact that you will be calling them to arrange a suitable time to meet up. Don't wait to be contacted as the recipients are usually busy people

4. Personal Marketing strategy

Just like a company develops a marketing plan for a product launch, you need to develop your own personal marketing strategy to market yourself. - after all you are the product to be marketed as the best solution to the needs of a company. An effective personal marketing plan is a working document which will usually contain the following elements:

- Your career objective – the position and industry you are looking to secure a position in.
- Elevator pitch – brief description of what expertise you can bring to an organization
- Reason for leaving or wanting to leave your current company
- Target companies and industries

- Examples of at least 8 achievements which relate to your core skills and competencies. This is a very useful exercise and is of great benefit to interview preparation.
- List your most valuable personal contacts that can provide career advice, CV / Resume feedback, input to personal marketing strategy and introductions to your target companies or other key network contacts.
-

Finally, be sure to proof-read your CV and cover letters. With today's technology there is no excuse for typo's, grammar or spelling mistakes. Don't underestimate the value of having someone else review your CV / Resume and cover letters.

Phase two – Go to market

Now that you have developed the foundations of your job search you should be ready to commence your job search campaign through effective networking, responding to job advertisements, contacting target companies and engaging with executive recruiters.

5. Effective networking

According to various sources of research, 70%-80% of jobs are now found through networking. Over 80% of jobs are never advertised. In many cases executives are appointed to positions which never come to the market. Just because you don't see an advertisement for a job or receive a phone call from an executive recruiter does not mean a company is not looking for you.

Networking is an extremely effective job search tool, and you need to be everywhere, both in person and online. Richard Branson's tip on networking is "early and often". Always arrive early to networking events and bring plenty of business cards. Practice your elevator pitch, career objective and reason for leaving prior to attending events or meeting networking contacts. Networking is extremely effective at uncovering the hidden job market; either to get connected to a key influencer in one of your target companies or being told the name of the executive recruiter who is handling a position with one of your target companies.

Job opportunities can be uncovered through networking with various sources e.g. lawyers, auditors, golf buddies, neighbours, university alumni, consultants and advisors. Each time you meet someone new; try to get them to provide you with names of 2-3 people who can provide you with introductions to your target organisations. When you meet these people, ask them for 2-3 names also and very quickly your network will expand rapidly.

One very important point that must be stressed - networking is about giving to get. It is not about taking, or just using people. Successful networking is figuring out what you can do for other people, not what they can do for you. Always say thank you to all those who have helped you and offer your help to them should they ever need it. If you approach networking in this manner you will find it extremely effective.

6. LinkedIn

By far the most popular professional social networking tool is LinkedIn. LinkedIn is your online CV. Make sure your profile is updated however If you don't want your employer and colleagues to know you are job searching then turn off the update notifications in settings.

Many people are unaware of the importance of the summary section of LinkedIn. The content you place in this section will show up in search engines e.g. Google and can also ensure you show up as a profile match to prospective employers and head-hunters when they advertise on LinkedIn. LinkedIn is a powerful tool – it is worth the time investment to get to know it either through your connections or watch some of the many online tutorials.

7. Engaging effectively with Executive recruiters

There are two types of executive recruiters; contingency recruiters (agencies) and retainer recruiters (Executive Search) and it is important to know the difference. Both are paid by the employer however contingency recruiters are only paid if and when someone they submit is actually hired. Retainer recruiters on the other hand are paid by the employer regardless of whether anyone they submit is actually hired. Instead they are compensated for their professional advice, skill and effort. One of the many reasons for choosing an executive search consultant is to conduct an external search while also considering internal candidates. The fact that they are paid anyway helps to ensure impartiality.

There are many factors to consider when dealing with executive recruiters some of which are outlined below:

- Recruiters are paid by the employer so this is where their loyalty lies - they will be interested in you if you can help them fill a position with their client.

- When making contact with executive recruiters be clear in terms of what position you are seeking.

- Offer to help them with candidate sourcing for any searches they may have. This helps build a relationship with the executive recruiter.

- Remember that most executive search companies will only tell you about one position at a time as it would be embarrassing for them if their clients were competing for the same shortlist. Given that the average search takes 3-4 months to complete then you are likely to be told of 2-3 positions per year from each executive search company. This is why networking is so important.

- Beware of some disgraceful if not illegal practices which occur within this sector which can become a stumbling block for many in finding the right career opportunity.
  - o If you receive a call from an executive recruiter telling you about a great opportunity, always checks that they really have the assignment. Many recruiters try to lure unsuspecting candidates with "let me represent you. I am a good friend of the CEO / HR Director" In many cases the truth is that that another recruiter has the assignment. The company then rejects the CV and the candidate can get locked out of the process. When the recruiter who has the assignment does eventually call the candidate the employer may not want to accept their CV in the

event there is a dispute over fees to two different recruiters.

o Another common practice is an individual responding to an advertisement for a position to be told that it has just been filled but to send their CV anyway as they have a similar assignment coming up soon. In many cases there was no such vacancy and the advert was an exercise to attract CV's which would be used to speculate to companies or worse still – to sell the valuable information contained in the CV to other companies.

8. Interview preparation

If you get to interview stage – well done! You have probably been shortlisted from a large number of other candidates and the skills and expertise you outlined on your CV / Resume have probably resonated with the hiring manager at some level. A positive attitude and mind-set is essential and equally important as demonstrating your skills and expertise. If you believe you can do the job then you must demonstrate this at the interview.

From the moment you introduce yourself at reception right through to the behaviours you demonstrate in the interview, your attitude and behaviours must exude those of a prospective employee. Be ready to fluently discuss your career objective, elevator pitch and reason for leaving your current position. Be prepared for tough interview questions. Know your past achievements and ensure you can substantiate each skill and area of expertise with an example.

Finally, cultural fit is as important as experience. There are many high profile examples of people who were fired or left organisations simply because they did not "fit". Many employers will be assessing this at interview and you should also do the same before, during and after the selection process.

Closing the deal / On-Boarding
9. Job contract and salary negotiation

Congratulations if you get to this stage and remember this could be the most valuable discussion you have during your job search!

Avoid premature conversations about salary during the interview process and instead try to keep the discussions focussed on what's really important – how you can add value to the company.

Although this may sound obvious, never quit your job until you have a written job offer from your prospective employer. The best way to secure a good deal from a prospective employer is to make them fully aware of the excellent salary and benefits package you have with your current employer. If you succeed in this then the initial offer should be something you can easily accept and will hopefully avoid unnecessary bargaining.

Preparing a summary of your current compensation package can be a useful exercise for managing expectations with recruiters and employers. Remember everything is negotiable so it is usually best to agree the salary first. Everything else can follow e.g. Bonus, Car, Health, Education etc.

In some situations it is possible to negotiate a termination agreement prior to joining which can provide for a period of extended notice or being kept on the payroll for a period of time after termination. This could be particularly valuable 10 years later when you could be in a higher position earning substantially more than when you joined.

10. On boarding – Reducing the time to competence
The first 6 months of any appointment is critical for both parties. The company wants evidence of added value from the new executive and the executive needs to feel that they have made the right career decision.

According to SHL it takes at least seven months for a new hire to be considered 'competent' in their new role! Seven months to get to a stage where they are no longer costing the organization money and are ready to start showing a return.

On-boarding coaching can help fast-track new executives to an advanced stage of productivity and engagement.

These programmes aim to align the new executives' talents with the employers' business objectives, inspire the executive to help meet those objectives and reinforce the decision made by employee and employer to join forces.

Benefits to the new executive:
- A confidential forum to discuss issues and courses of action.
- Gain an objective sounding board with a commercial and pragmatic approach to ensuring the success of the new relationship.
- Achieve individual and company objectives
- Obtain an independent appreciation and assessment of how to be instantly effective.

Benefits to the Company
- Release the potential of the new executive as quickly as possible.
- Build team awareness and the important networks of the new executive.
- Areas of stress between getting the job done and the new individual operating in an unfamiliar environment are quickly identified.
- Challenge the new recruit both on integration and adding value in the first 100 days.
- A new executive with clear objectives and a performance

11. Acknowledge people
Say thank you to all those who helped you during your job search campaign, let them know about your new appointment and offer your help to them should they ever need it. You never know when you may need their help again.

CONCLUSION

A well thought out job search strategy will be far more effective than one which is reactionary and lacks proactivity.

I regular say to my career coaching clients that looking for a job is a full time job and there is a direct correlation to the time put into job hunting and the success gained. To summarize:-

1. **Apply to organisations, not jobs**. "Don't just spend time looking for jobs that match your expertise and experience. Instead, identify good organisations that you want to work for. If you hear about a company that has a vision, mission, ambition, culture and product that appeals to you then research it. That's the best use of your time – not surfing internet job boards.

2. **Get connected – in person and online**. Get involved in professional organisations and attend conferences. Ensure the senior people in the industries you are interested in, including executive recruiters, know who you are. These will be the people that will help you ahead of your competition.

3. **Become top of mind to Executive Recruiters**. Ensure your CV / Resume attracts their attention.

4. **Demonstrate the benefit you bring**. "Organisations are not looking for job hunters – they want people who will bring bottom line benefit to their organisation. When you go to interview make sure you can demonstrate how you can add value to their business.

5. **Accept the right job – not any job**. Don't accept the first job offer until you are satisfied it is the right career move for you. One of the main reasons people recommence job hunting quickly is that they take any job rather than the right job.

Finally, two very useful books I recommend to my career coaching clients are:

1. **"Rites of Passage"** by John Lucht
2. **"Power Networking"** by Donna Fisher & Sandy Vilas

I hope this article has been of use to you and I wish you every success with your job search and future career.

About Hicks Kimber Mears

Hicks Kimber Mears are specialists in Executive Search who identify, assess and secure high quality people for Board and Senior / Middle management positions.

One of our key differentiators is finding talent that adds value quickly to our clients' bottom line rather than just filling the vacancy.

We operate from five offices – Dublin, London, Paris, Bristol and Munich - and over the last twenty years have gained an impressive reputation with a global client base. We are truly international and have the ability to recruit across cultures and countries which we handle in-house without the need to use third party networks where priorities and briefing are not necessarily aligned. Cantrell and Cochrane is an example of one of our long term clients where we placed over 140 Directors and Managers globally in the last 10 years.

About the Author: *Ken McIntyre-Barn is Managing Director of Hicks Kimber Mears in Ireland. Ken spent the first 14 years of his career working for well-known multinational organizations such as Unilever, Heineken, Wella and Kellogg's in Ireland, UK and Middle East ultimately reaching the position of Sales Director.*

Ken began his Consultancy career with a major global consultancy that specializes in helping clients sustainably change their organizations through practical but transformational solutions. He has considerable experience in strategy development, re-structuring, turnaround situations and sales force effectiveness. Ken is also a business advisor to nominated clients of Enterprise Ireland's International Selling program.

Throughout his career Ken gained considerable experience of talent acquisition and development of various cultures at senior level. Ken is also a Career Transition Coach, providing career coaching to executives who are in career transition or planning to change jobs. He has a Diploma in Coaching, is a practitioner in DISC, and is accredited in Occupational Testing by the British Psychological Society.

23. Time Management: A Blueprint to a Successful Life by *Severine Parker*

EXECUTIVE SUMMARY

I wish I had enough time! If I had enough time I would... have a successful business, relationship, life... complete as you see fit! Most of us blame our lack of time for our failure to do something or do something successfully. But is it really? Or is it our approach to time that creates those limitations? Moreover this relationship we have with time, the need we feel to have more time in order to do more, only creates more stress and reduces effectiveness.

Time Management is one of the many buzz words used in today's society. With the advent of modern technologies and the 24/7 availability motto, people have problems to switch off from their workplace. We can improve the quality of our work and eventually our productivity by deciding to do the things we do now, better and yielding more benefits. This is achieved by improving our relationship to time and our understanding on how we manage ourselves. Ultimately you only have 24 hours a day and that is the same for everybody so it is essential that we stop trying to always fit more in and keep real.

People are all very different and lead different lives, with different obligations and responsibilities, therefore it is naive to think it is possible to develop a system that would fit everyone. Only guidelines are possible. No matter what system you decide to follow, you will always need to adapt part of it to suit your own needs: you will have made it your own. In this article, I decided to concentrate on the key steps to follow in order to enable the making of an individual's blueprint to success.

In the article that follows I have highlighted the steps needed in order for you to draft your blueprint to success. It is important to do your research and work from the inside-out, which means that it starts with knowing yourself, your values and the carving of your vision.

You need to know your environment and how it impacts your vision and your actions. Planning and prioritizing are an important part of the process but are not worth much without action. The human tendency to procrastinate can hinder our time management as can interruptions but there are ways to handle these. Finally no process is ever finished without regular review.

And so while the steps highlighted in this article can be applied to using time management techniques to improve business efficiencies and making a business more successful, they need to be applied to an individual's life as a whole. However it is recommended to follow a gradual approach in order to avoid burn out and failure, the keys being perseverance and consistency.

To manage your time to the best effect, i.e. lead a successful life where success is not synonymous with wealth but with how satisfied and happy you are with your life, to be in control of your time, to manage your time effectively, you need to apply the principles to both your professional life and your personal life, i.e. to your life as a whole. Only when you master the integrated approach to time management are you really in control of your time and your life and well on the way to success!

INTRODUCTION

In our modern world of technology and being switched on 24/7, stress is now such an important factor, creating so many dysfunctions, let them be physical, mental, interpersonal and making even the most successful person (in financial terms that is) feel miserable, that most media now speaks or report about some theme or other linked to Time Management which is seen as the key to better productivity or the key to work /life balance, depending on which approach you take.

Everybody wants to be happy, or at least happier, and a lot of people are looking for the secrets of the people they perceived as successful. The thing is that what works for one person does not always work for another.

However, fear not, a blueprint exists in order to figure out how to improve yourself in order to improve your life. I can hear you now *"but I don't want to improve myself I want to manage my time better"*. The thing is you can't control time. Time is an abstract notion created by humans. We all have the same 24 hours. It's our use of these hours that determines how successful we are. By successful, I do not mean how much money you have or earn, though for quite a few people it is the main criteria of success, but more how satisfied you are with your life as a whole.

You need to change your relationship to time and above all your beliefs and actions, i.e. you need to change things inside-out. And it starts with you. You need to understand yourself better: who you are, what you want, how you react to particular situations, where you want to be in 1, 5, or 10 years' time. You need to have a vision, a purpose with clear measurable goals, and sub-steps. You need to understand what motivates people in general, but most importantly people that are a big part of your life, as their happiness is also part of the picture. What they want, how they react is also part of your blueprint (let it be your boss, clients, colleagues, your husband, wife, kids, etc). It's all related. We do not live in a vacuum so it is important that we concentrate on the inter-relationships that exist between our success/happiness and that of others around us.

For this you need a written plan, not just for your career, but for your life as a whole. It's only by tackling both your professional life and your personal life that you will have a chance to be truly successful whatever that word encompasses for you. Only when you master the integrated approach to time management are you really in control of your time and your life. For this, you need self-discipline and courage.

In the article that follows I have highlighted the 5 steps needed in order for you to draft your blueprint to success.

DO YOUR RESEARCH!

Before you start on your journey to develop an efficient and effective you, you need to stop and do some background research! You need to make sure you focus on the right tasks, values, activities, learning, etc. and that they all fit your overall vision. Don't forget the well-known idiom: knowledge is power and without this knowledge you will not reach the full potential of control on your time and your life

Where should you be spending your time both in your professional and personal life?

In order to determine this, you first need to define your purpose in life, your vision!

Most people want to be happy but what does it entail for you. What do you want out of life? Where do you see yourself in 1, 5, 10 years' time? You need to know exactly where you're going in order to get there, otherwise, how will you know when you're there? It seems obvious but most people just want to get things done and don't really spend a great deal of time in thinking about where exactly they're heading or even why they are doing particular tasks. You are always more efficient if you work towards a precise goal with a definite timeline.

One word of caution though, be sure your vision is achievable and measurable otherwise if you ignore your capabilities you might set yourself up for failure, dissatisfaction and unhappiness.

... you also need to know your environment, i.e. your stakeholders...

Humans, intrinsically, are social beings and they live in a world where everything is inter-related. So you need to be aware of the influence of your stakeholders on your life and to understand your stakeholders' needs and wants. For this you need to ask questions! It might seem obvious but a lot of people assume they know...and unfortunately they don't always assume correctly.

Your biggest stakeholder is often considered to be where your living comes from. Usually this is the company you work for. If you don't know them already, find out your company's mission statement, vision, short-term and long-term goals. You need to know this in order to figure out how working for this particular company influences your own career/life plan. Also by knowing your company's objectives and priorities, you can determine how you can be more efficient by highlighting the activities you have to prioritise for maximum impact.

Two other major stakeholders in an individual's life are usually their family and friends. Very often imbalance and unhappiness happen when one or both are ignored. Too many people, when looking at time management, only concentrate on their primary stakeholder, as ranked in monetary values, and ignore or don't make time for the others. Unfortunately, our emotional support network (family and friends) is often what makes or breaks our happiness scale.

Once you understand your environment, it becomes easier to comprehend how it fits with your vision and what steps need to be taken in order to make your work more effective and also how to use your environment to help you reach your vision. What are the high yield tasks of your job? What activities create the most benefits (not just in monetary terms) to your stakeholders? You need to concentrate on them. And don't forget, as people/organisations are ever changing, this needs to be done on a continuous basis.

...and finally, you need to know where you actually spend your time

Once you've done that, you need to keep a diary for a week or so to find out where, at present, you are actually spending your time and how long it takes you to do certain activities. We all think we know that one and yet people are always surprised at the result of this exercise.

WHAT ARE THE THREE MOST IMPORTANT ACTIVITIES THAT GENERATE THE GREATEST RETURNS FOR YOU? AND HOW MUCH TIME DO YOU SPEND IN THESE ACTIVITIES IN TOTAL PER DAY/WEEK?

The method recommended to track where you spend your time varies from tracking every time you shift your attention to recording every 5 minutes, half an hour, hour... I wouldn't advise more than that as you rarely remember every detail and unfortunately little tasks can add up to quite a chunk at the end of the week. Don't stop tracking once you leave the office. A lot of people, above all if you own your business, don't have regular working hours and keep taking professional phone calls in their personal time. To manage your life as a whole you need to track your time at home too.

Tracking your time is also useful to see the level of interruptions you are exposed to and the amount of procrastination smothering your life...

Once you know your environment, how you are spending your time and above all where you *should* be spending it, you can then start with the planning.

FAIL TO PLAN AND PLAN TO FAIL: TAKE CONTROL OF YOUR DAY

To plan you need to prioritise your tasks judging their importance and urgency. Ask questions when you are given a task to make sure you are clear. Assumptions can create uncertainties and this makes you less efficient. The more urgent and important a task is the higher on the list it should be. Sometimes it requires weighing the pros and cons on doing a task over another in order to decide which one to do first. Sometimes it requires external decision-making from your most important stakeholder: your boss, client, family member, etc. What are the implications of not doing a task? Sometimes the result of doing a task may not seem very important nor urgent, however the consequences of not doing that task could mean the loss of a client or project as it may not be important for you but is for somebody else whose good will you would lose if this task is not done. And so, this fact could shoot that task to the top of your list.

Write it down. You need to have a clear picture in your head of what you need to do and why and that starts with writing it down! No matter how good you are with remembering things, having a written plan is always more efficient (nothing gets forgotten and it can be improved easily). Writing makes your ideas clearer and focuses you on your end result. It also makes you more accountable.

People are good at making lists but then it gets forgotten about, lost or seems to be never ending. Some professionals advise not to have a list. Plan your tasks in your calendar straightaway. No matter what, never do just a list of items without clearly marking in front of them a clear deadline. Make a list for 'one day maybes', things you would like to do – try to fit some of these into your action list from time to time so that you don't forget yourself as an individual. No matter what, you need to plan time in there to take care of yourself. Think of yourself as a machine if you have to. If the machine is not kept in good working order, it will eventually fail to do what you want it to do. Take care of yourself, eat well, rest, exercise. Socialise and have at least a couple of people you can let off steam with and have a laugh. All of this should be part of your plan.

You also need to plan with your abilities in mind, e.g. plan the easy more liked tasks for when you are less "awake" and keep the hard ones for when you are at your most efficient.

Harness the power of routine by blocking time for a particular task or type of tasks (project work, emails, phone calls). It will save time to batch like tasks together, increase your focus and, routinely doing something at the same time on the same day, helps fighting procrastination and can make some tasks seem less daunting after a while.

Finally, do a quick plan/to-do list the day before. This will stop you from mulling over and being afraid you will forget something, allowing you a more restful time off.

ORGANIZE YOUR ENVIORNMENT FOR EFFICIENCIES

Organise your desk. Declutter. Clearing your desk of all papers will remove distractions, temptations to do something else (above all if you don't really want to do what you have to do!). Put things back in their place as you've finished with them. If you do it as you go, it's easy but at the end of the day when you're tired and looking forward to go home, not so much, then it is often left there for LATER. Before you know it, you have a mountain of paper to file and no motivation to do so. You waste time looking for particular documents because in spite of what you say to your colleagues, you do not know where everything is. You might have an inkling that it's in that pile but..., or you just re-print it and add to your clutter! You should have a proper filing system in place. It doesn't have to be complicated, it has to suit you. If you have an assistant or a partner, it means they will be able to help you when you ring them when you forget something or you need help with a particular project because they will be able to find your notes and any related documents. For effective organising you need to follow the **4 D** rules often advocated by time management experts: **D**o it Now, **D**ump, **D**elegate, **D**efer. And that's also valid for your computer files and your emails too by the way! And all three systems should be identical.

Finally, follow the usual rules of ergonomics and desk/office organisation. Make sure your environment is comfortable (look at health and safety guidelines related to the workplace) and organised. Things should be placed in your office according to the use you make of them; the less you use them to further away from you they should be.

Action: Now you're all set, have your plan/to do list(s) displayed prominently where you can check it regularly (on your fridge, at your desk at work) either in paper form or in electronic form. The advantage of electronic form is that you can set reminders, share your calendars with other people, send invites, but make sure it's backed up. The advantage of paper form is that it's accessible at all time. Moreover having a calendar at home on the wall where everybody can see it is handy for improved family life. Everybody knows what everybody is doing. It limits the inconvenience of double-booking or forgetfulness.

You could have a great plan displayed, but if you don't act on it or don't act on it as planned, excluding necessary essential adjustments, then it won't be much good in helping you get control of your life. The main obstacles to actions and effectiveness are procrastination, multitasking, thinking you can do it all and interruptions.

Procrastination, "The Do It Now" principle: Procrastination is often created by anxiety, fear relating to the importance of the task, the perceived negatives of the task (boring, complex, time-consuming, difficult), perfectionism or a mix of all of these. Different methods are used to deal with this anxiety and other negative feelings: mindfulness, positive thinking, visualisation, rewarding... Difficult tasks can be made less unpleasant with a little attention to setting up our surroundings in order to make it more pleasant and also an awareness of our own mental state, what we are thinking/feeling at a certain time.

To list the motivation might kick start you in taking the first step. What will happen if you do it? What will you gain? If picturing the end result, remembering your vision and all the good you will get from sticking to your plan and getting on with the task on hand doesn't work then you might try to think about what would happen if you didn't do that particular task. What would you lose? Depending on your state of mind, you could get motivated by the positive or the negative. The problem with the negative is that sometime it delivers a pressure/stress that paralyses us and renders us unable to act. Figure out what works for you. Sometimes you just need to get your act together and 'just do it'! You are not a kid anymore and there are things in life that just have to get done. You probably know the Chinese adage of the longest journey starting with a single step. So break the main task down into smaller more manageable tasks and stick to your plan, one task at a time. Good planning helps fight procrastination.

Finally for something to be "good enough" is sometimes... enough! Human beings are very good at adding complexity to the simplest thing. Perfectionism can freeze you in your tracks, unleashing anxiety and self-doubt. It is important to concentrate first on getting the task done then worry about improving it if you can. "Perfection is the enemy of good" especially when it prevents you from starting! Focusing on starting tasks rather than completing them can also help in avoiding procrastination.

Focus on one thing at a time: Multitasking, attempting to complete many tasks at one time, is listed as a requirement in many job descriptions along with effective time management and there are still many companies that view the ability to multitask as being a proof of better productivity. However most experts in time management systems view multitasking as a limiting factor and agree that focusing on one task at a time is an essential condition of successful time management. It has been proven in numerous research studies that the brain cannot fully focus when multitasking and as a result people take longer to complete tasks and are more prone to error. Unfortunately, there are jobs where you have no choice but to multitask to the best of your ability and it is true that some people seem better at handling multitasking than others. However whenever possible, multitasking should only be exercised in case of absolute necessity and processes should be put in place to limit the need for multitasking.

Interruptions: In order to foster focus, you need to remove or at least limit interruptions to urgent/important tasks. Remove email notification or better, close your email application, divert your phone to voice mail, mute your phone so you don't hear it ring, put a 'do not disturb' sign on the door... Whatever is necessary!

Strive to separate your personal life from your professional life, and their respective issues, as much as possible, in order to promote focused and quality time. This will enable you to better recharge your batteries and will limit the risk of neglecting one over the other.

Just say no or... say, I can't do it right now but I can do it later, tomorrow, next week. Be firm and assertive. Sometimes these tasks then disappear. Helping people is great and by all means do it if you can but not if it is detrimental to your own goals and happiness. That's when prioritising and being able to weigh pros and cons are essential.

Take charge & Delegate: Nobody is irreplaceable and doing everything yourself is not going to make you so. On the contrary, it could be your biggest pitfall for your career. Make sure you are the right person to do the task. Could somebody else do it better and faster than you? Would your time be more valuably used on some other possibly higher yield task?

And giving credit where credit is due shows you as a team player and will ensure you always get the best help. Be nice and polite! Give specific directions. Be concise, but not overly so, if you want the job done more or less as you want it. It might not be as you would have done it but it might be good enough!

1. Review

Even if you think you have it down pat, if you rest on your laurels you might fall back into old habits little by little without noticing. Moreover, like for everything else in life, nothing ever stays the same so why should your habits! You have to revisit the way you do things regularly to make sure you're still on track and also adjust your aim as your goal changes. Do your own audit!

CONCLUSION

Successful time management is essential to develop a successful business but not just. A lot of books and articles are written on the subject but there is no right or wrong system. It's all about trial and error. It is a long process requiring self-discipline. You cannot control time, nobody does, you can only control the way you use it and so it all boils down to YOU. Self-discipline can be considered a type of selective training. You need to create new habits of thought, action, and speech in order to improve yourself and reach your goals. The change starts with your thinking. You have to know what's important for you, you have to commit and prioritise and dedicate time to develop your blueprint and act on it.

Like any skills you learn it takes time and work but it's worth it and can make a huge difference to your life. You have to give it time, this is not an overnight miracle though some of the advice here when implemented, will give immediate results, but unless you are willing to put in the work necessary in doing your research, planning, acting on your plan and reviewing your plan regularly, you will never reach the status of successful time management.

Above all you have to remember that you don't need to implement the whole lot at once: one small step at a time! You might sometimes feel that you're going backward when first embarking on this journey and you might perceive a short-term loss of time but you have to persevere and focus on the long-term goal: making your business a successful one and gaining control of your life! Perseverance and consistency are keys. Keep trying and keep doing it regularly (same day, same time, every day is best). Try your best, but expect a few bumps along the way.

Slow and steady win the race... Small steps will ensure you build your confidence over time and are better armed at facing harder tasks with a more positive outlook. Don't try and implement the whole lot at once this only leads to frustration and resentment, discouragement and in the end failure. And you will say "this system does not work" or "this is rubbish". You won't know for sure unless you give it a chance. In the end, with trying this system and that, you will end up with your very own blueprint. Your blueprint for a successful business and most importantly, your blueprint for a successful life!

REFERENCES

Allen, D., 2001. *Getting Things Done: The Art of Stress-Free Productivity*. Penguin Books.

Covey, S., 2004. *The 7 Habits of Highly Effective People*. 2nd Ed. Simon & Schuster.

Dood, P. & Sundheim, D., 2008. *The 25Best Time Management Tools & Techniques*. 2nd Ed. Capstone Publishing.

Evans, C., 2008. *Time Management for Dummies*. John Wiley & Sons.

MacKenzie, A., 1997. *The Time Trap: The Classic Book on Time Management*. 3rd Ed. Amacom.

Manser, M., 2010. *Time Managements Secrets.* Collins.
Tracy, B., 2001. *Eat that frog! 21 Great Ways to Stop Procrastinating and Get More Done in Less Time*. Berrett-Koehler Publishers.

Walsh, R., 2008. *Time Management: Proven Techniques for Making Every Minute Count*. 2nd Ed. Adams Business.
Zeigler, K., 2008. *Getting organised at work: 24 lessons to set goals, establish priorities and manage your time*. McGraw Hill Professional.

About the Author: *A French native, living in Ireland, Severine has a diverse educational and professional background. Her career journey has included software engineering, senior administration, and entrepreneurial start-ups.*

As a research assistant to the Director of the Centre for Applied Language Studies in the University of Limerick, she was instrumental in the publication of a Corpus of Journalistic French for Oxford University.

Her current new business ventures are **A La Carte PA** *(which offers bespoke administrative support to small businesses and individuals on an hourly basis or through a cost effective retainer package. Services include but are not limited to, secretarial, email and diary management, travel organization and event management) www.alacartepa.ie and **A La Carte French** (which offers French/English translation services and French Language courses for both businesses and individuals) www.alacartefrench.ie.*

Severine has a Business Degree specializing in Hotel & Catering Management, a Graduate Diploma in Computing and a Master's Degree in French.

REFERENCES

Fund & Follow Creativity [Online] (2012) Available: http://www.kickstarter.com/ (last accessed Aug. 28, 2012).

Agnda, H., and Nilsson, U.,(2009). *Interorganisational cost management in the exchange process*, Management Accounting Research 20: 85-101

Allen, D., (2001). *Getting Things Done: The Art of Stress-Free Productivity*. Penguin Books

Avgerou,C.,Ciborra,C.,and Land, F.F, editors (2004). **The Social Study of Information and Communication Technology: Innovation, Actors and Context** Oxford, OUP

Blanchard,B and Fabrycky,W, (2010). **Systems Engineering and Analysis**, Fifth Edition, Prentice Hall, 2010

Central Statistics Office (2012) *Business in Ireland 2009*
Collins, J. (2004) *'Good to Great'*. USA: Random House Business Books

Connor, M. and Pokora, J. (2007). **'Coaching and mentoring at work: developing effective practice'**. England: McGraw-Hill
Copeland, Michael V (2006). *How to Find your Angel*, Business 2.0; Mar2006, Vol. 7 Issue 2, p47-49, 3p,

Covey, S.,(2004). *The 7 Habits of Highly Effective People*. 2nd Ed. Simon & Schuster.

CSO: Census of Population Data, (2006).

CSO: Population and Migration Estimates 2003 and 2006

Dood, P., and Sundheim, D., (2008). *The 25Best Time Management Tools & Techniques*. 2nd Ed. Capstone Publishing.

Evans, C.,(2008). **Time Management for Dummies**. John Wiley & Sons.

Franke, N., Venture Capitalists' **Evaluations of Start-Up Teams: Trade-Offs, Knock-Out Criteria, and the Impact of VC Experience**.

Garvey Berger, J. (2012). *'Changing on the Job'*, California: Stanford University Press

Goldratt, E., **Haystack Syndrome**, North River Press, 1990.

Goleman D. et al (2002). *'The New Leaders',* USA: Harvard Business School Press

Heifetz, R et al. (2009). *'The Practice of Adaptive Leadership'* USA: Harvard Business School Publishing

Gruber, F. (2011) *Top 8 European Startup Accelerators And Incubators Ranked: Seedcamp And Startup Bootcamp Top The Rankings* [Online] Available: http://tech.co/top-8-european-startup-accelerators-and-incubators-ranked-seedcamp-and-startup-bootcamp-top-the-rankings-2011-06.

Henderson, G., (1994). **Cultural Diversity in the workplace: Issues and Strategies**, Praeger Westport, CT.

Hobman, E.V., et Al.(2004*). Perceived Dissimilarity and work group involvement : the moderating effects of group openness to diversity*, Group and Organization Management, Vol. 29, No. 5,560-588

Hofstede, G., (2001), **Culture's Consequences**, Sage, Thousand Oaks.

Hopp, W.and Spearman,M , (2011). **Factory Physics**, Waveland Press

IAB Pricewaterhouse Coopers Online (2009-2010*). Adspend Survey*

Kandola, R., and Fullerton, J., (1994), **Managing the mosaic: Diversity in Action**, Institute of Personal Development, London.

Kossiakoff, A and Sweet, W, (2003). **Systems Engineering Principles and Practice**. Wiley-Interscience,

Maass, E., and McNair, P., (2009**). Applying Design for Six Sigma to Software and Hardware Systems,** Prentice-Hall.

Manser, M., (2010). **Time Managements Secrets**. Collins.

McMillan-Capehart, A.,(2006*), Heterogeneity or Homogeneity: Socialization makes the difference in firm performance*, Performance Improvement Quarterly, Vol. 19 No.1, 83.

MacKenzie, A., (1997). **The Time Trap: The Classic Book on Time Management**. 3rd Ed. Amacom.

O'Leary, P (2009) 'The Personality Characteristics of Ireland's Most Successful Entrepreneurs', unpublished, Trinity College Dublin.

Passmore, W (1988). ***Designing Effective Organizations***: The Sociotechnical Systems Perspective, John WIley & Sons.

Ries, E. (2011) *The Lean Startup: How Today's Entrepreneurs Use Continuous Innovation to Create Radically Successful Businesses*, New York: Random House.
Rodriguez, R., (2006). **Diversity finds its place,** HR Magazine vol. 51, No. 8.

Rosinski, P., (2003. **COACHING ACROSS CULTURES**, Nicholas Brealey Publishing.

Shel Isreal: (2009).*Twitterville*: It's about "telling" rather than "selling"'

Tracy, B., 2001. **Eat that frog! 21 Great Ways to Stop Procrastinating and Get More Done in Less Time.** Berrett-Koehler Publishers.

Thomas, D.A., and Ely, R.J., (1996), **Making Differences Matter**, Harvard Business Review, Vol. 74, No. 5, 79-90.

Touraine, A., (2000), **Can we live together? Equality and difference**, Stanford University Press, Stanford

Walsh, R., (2008). **Time Management: Proven Techniques for Making Every Minute Count**. 2nd Ed. Adams Business.

Womack,J., Jones,D., Roos,*D*., (1991). **The Machine That Changed the World : The Story of Lean Production,** Harper Perennial.

Zeigler, K., (2008)**. Getting organised at work: 24 lessons to set goals, establish priorities and manage your time.** McGraw Hill Professional

WEB BIBLIOGRAPHY

www.forfas.ie/media/260412 The Irish Enterprise Funding Environment-publication.pdf
www.djei.ie/enterprise/smes/publications.htm
www.djei.ie/enterprise/smes/RIACredit_Guarantee_Scheme.pdf
www.enterpriseboards.ie
www.enterprise-ireland.com
www.first-step.ie
www.hban.org
www.idaireland.com
www.intertradeireland.com
www.irishleadernetwork.org
www.revenue.ie
www.aibseedcapitalfund.ie
www.businessbanking.bankofireland.com/loans/seed-and-early-stage-fund
www.ivca.ie

www.enterprise.gov.ie/Publications/Financial-Support-for-Irish-Business.pdf
www.revenue.ie/en/tax/it/leaflets/it15.html)
www.revenue.ie/en/tax/it/leaflets/new-it55-e11.pdf
www.revenue.ie/en/tax/ct/research-development.html
www.innovationvouchers.ie
www.seai.ie/Your_Business/Accelerated_Capital_Allowance
www.revenue.ie/en/tax/it/leaflets/it59.html
www.welfare.ie/en/schemes/jobseekersupports/backtowork/empl
oyerjobprsiincentivescheme/Pages/Emp_PRSI.aspx
www.jobbridge.ie
www.connectireland.com
www.djei.ie/press/2011/20110510d.htm
www.djei.ie/press/2012/20120411.htm
www.creditreview.ie
www.skillnets.ie
www.failteireland.ie
www.kickstarter.com
www.cynthiakocialski.com/blog/2010/09/16/why-few-start-ups-build-the-fundable-dream-team/
www.sociotechical.org/archive.htm
www.sociotechnical.org
wwwessex ac.uk/chimera
www.CoachingAcrossCultures.com Rosinski, P.
Management Development Council (2010) *'Management Development in Ireland'*
www.forfas.ie/media/100316mdc-management-development-in-ireland.pdf
Industry Week.com (2010) *'Leadership in Manufacturing'*
www.industryweek.com/PrintArticle.aspx?ArticleID=26148&ShowAll=1&SectionID=2
Intertrade Ireland (2009) Management Matters in Northern Ireland and Republic of Ireland
www.intertradeireland.com/media/intertradeirelandcom/researc
handstatistics/publications/tradeandbusinessdevelopment/Mana
gement%20matters%20in%20Northern%20Ireland%20and%2
0Republic%20of%20Ireland.pdf
www.irishpatents.ie
www.patentsoffice.ie
www.uspto.gov

www.epo.org
www.enterprise-ireland.com
www.marketresearch.com
www.patentsoffice.ie
www.kompass.com
www.dnb.co.uk
www.statistics.gov.uk
www.census.gov
www.cso.ie

VIDEOS
Iain McGilchrist (2011) *The Divided Brain.* UK, RSA; RSA Animate
www.comment.rsablogs.org.uk/2011/10/24/rsa-animate-divided-brain/

Dan Pink (2010) 'Drive'. UK: RSA; RSA Animate
www.youtube.com/watch?v=u6XAPnuFjJc

WALKER*PUBLICATIONS

Walker Publications specializes in unique writers with innovative approaches to topics. Novice and experienced authors find the Walker process simple with a responsive staff to assist in the journey of publishing.

Poised at the leading edge of the "*New Way to Conduct Business*", Walker writers blend mind, body, and spirit in the essence of their writing to deliver holistic relevant works for individuals, groups, and organizations.

.

Walker*Publications
T: 480-262-1523
E: ideas@walkerpublications.co
W: www.walkerpublications.co

Made in the USA
San Bernardino, CA
04 December 2012